Manhattan Review

Test Prep & Admissions Consulting

Turbocharge Your GRE: Sets, Statistics & Data Interpretation Guide

part of the 3rd Edition Series

April 20th, 2016

- ☐ *100 GRE-like practice questions*
  - *Multiple Choice - 55 Questions*
  - *Select One or Many - 15 Questions*
  - *Numeric Entry - 15 Questions*
  - *Quantitative Comparison - 15 Questions*
- ☐ *Questions mapped according to the scope of the GRE*
- ☐ *Ample number of questions with Alternate Approaches*
- ☐ *Text-cum-graphic explanations of concepts*

www.manhattanreview.com

Copyright and Terms of Use

Copyright and Trademark

Terms of Use

No Warranties

Limitation on Liability

10-Digit International Standard Book Number: (ISBN: 1-62926-080-0)
13-Digit International Standard Book Number: (ISBN: 978-1-62926-080-8)

Last updated on April 20th, 2016.

Manhattan Review, 275 Madison Avenue, Suite 1429, New York, NY 10016.
Phone: +1 (212) 316-2000. E-Mail: info@manhattanreview.com. Web: www.manhattanreview.com

About the Turbocharge your GRE Series

The Turbocharge Your GRE Series consists of 13 guides that cover everything you need to know for a great score on the GRE. Widely respected among GRE educators worldwide, Manhattan Review's GRE prep books offer the most professional GRE instruction available anywhere. Now in its updated 3rd edition, the full series is carefully designed to provide GRE test-takers with exhaustive GRE preparation for optimal test scores. Manhattan Review's GRE prep books teach you how to prepare for each of the different GRE testing areas with a thorough instructional methodology that is rigorous yet accessible and enjoyable. You'll learn everything necessary about each test section in order to receive your best possible GRE scores. The full series covers GRE verbal, quantitative, and writing concepts from the most basic through the most advanced levels, and is therefore a great study resource for all stages of GRE preparation. Students who work through all books in the series significantly improve their knowledge of GRE subject matter and learn the most strategic approaches to taking and vanquishing the GRE.

GRE Math Essentials Guide (ISBN: 978-1-62926-073-0)
- ☐ **GRE Number Properties Guide (ISBN: 978-1-62926-074-7)**
- ☐ **GRE Arithmetic Guide (ISBN: 978-1-62926-075-4**
- ☐ **GRE Algebra Guide (ISBN: 978-1-62926-076-1**
- ☐ **GRE Geometry Guide (ISBN: 978-1-62926-077-8)**
- ☐ **GRE Word Problems Guide (ISBN: 978-1-62926-078-5)**
- ☐ **GRE Combinatorics & Probability Guide (ISBN: 978-1-62926-079-2)**
- ■ **GRE Sets, Statistics & Data Interpretation Guide (ISBN: 978-1-62926-080-8)**
- ☐ **GRE Quantitative Question Bank (ISBN: 978-1-62926-081-5)**
- ☐ **GRE Reading Comprehension Guide (ISBN: 978-1-62926-082-2)**
- ☐ **GRE Sentence Equivalence & Text Completion Guide (ISBN: 978-1-62926-083-9)**
- ☐ **GRE Analytical Writing Guide (ISBN: 978-1-62926-084-6)**
- ☐ **GRE Vocabulary Builder (ISBN: 978-1-62926-085-3)**

About the Company

Manhattan Review's origin can be traced directly back to an Ivy League MBA classroom in 1999. While teaching advanced quantitative subjects to MBAs at Columbia Business School in New York City, Professor Dr. Joern Meissner developed a reputation for explaining complicated concepts in an understandable way. Prof. Meissner's students challenged him to assist their friends, who were frustrated with conventional test preparation options. In response, Prof. Meissner created original lectures that focused on presenting standardized test content in a simplified and intelligible manner, a method vastly different from the voluminous memorization and so-called tricks commonly offered by others. The new methodology immediately proved highly popular with students, inspiring the birth of Manhattan Review.

Since its founding, Manhattan Review has grown into a multi-national educational services firm, focusing on preparation for the major undergraduate and graduate admissions tests, college admissions consulting, and application advisory services, with thousands of highly satisfied students all over the world. Our GRE material is continuously expanded and updated by the Manhattan Review team, an enthusiastic group of master GRE professionals and senior academics. Our team ensures that Manhattan Review offers the most time-efficient and cost-effective preparation available for the GRE. Please visit www.ManhattanReview.com for further details.

About the Founder

Professor Dr. Joern Meissner has more than 25 years of teaching experience at the graduate and undergraduate levels. He is the founder of Manhattan Review, a worldwide leader in test prep services, and he created the original lectures for its first test preparation classes. Prof. Meissner is a graduate of Columbia Business School in New York City, where he received a PhD in Management Science. He has since served on the faculties of prestigious business schools in the United Kingdom and Germany. He is a recognized authority in the areas of supply chain management, logistics, and pricing strategy. Prof. Meissner thoroughly enjoys his research, but he believes that grasping an idea is only half of the fun. Conveying knowledge to others is even more fulfilling. This philosophy was crucial to the establishment of Manhattan Review, and remains its most cherished principle.

The Advantages of Using Manhattan Review

- **Time efficiency and cost effectiveness.**
  - For most people, the most limiting factor of test preparation is time.
  - It takes significantly more teaching experience to prepare a student in less time.
  - Our test preparation approach is tailored for busy professionals. We will teach you what you need to know in the least amount of time.
- **Our high-quality and dedicated instructors are committed to helping every student reach her/his goals.**

International Phone Numbers and Official Manhattan Review Websites

Manhattan Headquarters	+1-212-316-2000	www.manhattanreview.com
USA & Canada	+1-800-246-4600	www.manhattanreview.com
Argentina	+1-212-316-2000	www.review.com.ar
Australia	+61-3-9001-6618	www.manhattanreview.com
Austria	+43-720-115-549	www.review.at
Belgium	+32-2-808-5163	www.manhattanreview.be
Brazil	+1-212-316-2000	www.manhattanreview.com.br
Chile	+1-212-316-2000	www.manhattanreview.cl
China	+86-20-2910-1913	www.manhattanreview.cn
Czech Republic	+1-212-316-2000	www.review.cz
France	+33-1-8488-4204	www.review.fr
Germany	+49-89-3803-8856	www.review.de
Greece	+1-212-316-2000	www.review.com.gr
Hong Kong	+852-5808-2704	www.review.hk
Hungary	+1-212-316-2000	www.review.co.hu
India	+1-212-316-2000	www.review.in
Indonesia	+1-212-316-2000	www.manhattanreview.id
Ireland	+1-212-316-2000	www.gmat.ie
Italy	+39-06-9338-7617	www.manhattanreview.it
Japan	+81-3-4589-5125	www.manhattanreview.jp
Malaysia	+1-212-316-2000	www.review.my
Mexico	+1-212-316-2000	www.manhattanreview.mx
Netherlands	+31-20-808-4399	www.manhattanreview.nl
New Zealand	+1-212-316-2000	www.review.co.nz
Philippines	+1-212-316-2000	www.review.ph
Poland	+1-212-316-2000	www.review.pl
Portugal	+1-212-316-2000	www.review.pt
Qatar	+1-212-316-2000	www.review.qa
Russia	+1-212-316-2000	www.manhattanreview.ru
Singapore	+65-3158-2571	www.gmat.sg
South Africa	+1-212-316-2000	www.manhattanreview.co.za
South Korea	+1-212-316-2000	www.manhattanreview.kr
Sweden	+1-212-316-2000	www.gmat.se
Spain	+34-911-876-504	www.review.es
Switzerland	+41-435-080-991	www.review.ch
Taiwan	+1-212-316-2000	www.gmat.tw
Thailand	+66-6-0003-5529	www.manhattanreview.com
Turkey	+1-212-316-2000	www.review.com.tr
United Arab Emirates	+1-212-316-2000	www.manhattanreview.ae
United Kingdom	+44-20-7060-9800	www.manhattanreview.co.uk
Rest of World	+1-212-316-2000	www.manhattanreview.com

Contents

Chapter 1

Welcome

Dear Students,

Here at Manhattan Review, we constantly strive to provide you the best educational content for standardized test preparation. We make a tremendous effort to keep making things better and better for you. This is especially important with respect to an examination such as the GRE. A typical GRE aspirant is confused with so many test-prep options available. Your challenge is to choose a book or a tutor that prepares you for attaining your goal. We cannot say that we are one of the best, it is you who has to be the judge.

There are umpteen numbers of books on Quantitative Reasoning for GRE preparation. What is so different about this book? The answer lies in its approach to deal with the questions. Solution of each question is dealt with in detail. Quite a handful number of questions have been solved through Alternate Approaches. The objective is to understand questions from multiple aspects. The book has a great collection of 100 GRE-like questions.

Apart from books on 'Number Properties,' 'Word Problem,' 'Algebra,' 'Arithmetic,' 'Geometry,' 'Combinatorics & Probability,' and 'Sets, Statistics and Data Interpretation' which are solely dedicated to GRE-Quantitative Reasoning, the book on 'GRE-Math Essentials' is solely dedicated to develop your math fundamentals.

The Manhattan Review's 'GRE-Sets, Statistics and Data Interpretation' book is holistic and comprehensive in all respects. Should you have any queries, feel free to write to me at info@manhattanreview.com.

Happy Learning!

Professor Dr. Joern Meissner
& The Manhattan Review Team

Chapter 2

Concepts

2.1 Sets

A Set is a collection of well-defined things. The objects of a set are called its elements or members.

Nomenclature:

- **Universal Set:** All sets are assumed to be contained in a set called the universal set.
- **Null Set:** An empty set having no elements in it is called a null set.
- **Disjoint Set**: Two sets are disjoint if they have no elements in common.
  For example: $A = \{1, 2, 3\}$ and $B = \{4, 5, 6\}$ are two disjoint sets.
- **Cardinal Number of a Set:** The Cardinal number of a finite set A is the number of elements of the set, denoted by $n(A)$. For example: For $A = \{1, 2, 3\}, n(A) = 3$

Venn Diagrams: A Venn diagram is a pictorial representation of sets represented by enclosed areas in a plane. The universal set is represented by a rectangle, and the other sets are represented by areas lying within it.

Set Operations:

- **Union:** The Union of two sets A and B, i.e. $A \cup B$, is a set that contains all the elements contained in set A or set B.

  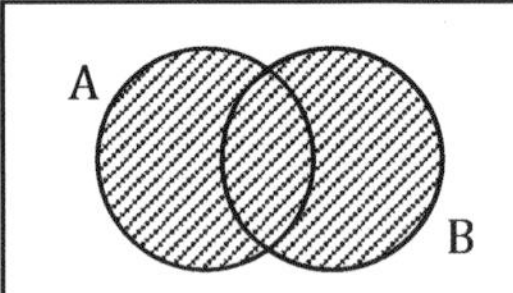

  For example: If $A = \{2, 3\}, B = \{1, 3, 5\}$

  $\Rightarrow A \cup B = \{1, 2, 3, 5\}$

- **Intersection:** Intersection of two sets A and B, i.e. $A \cap B$, that contains the elements common to both sets A and B.

  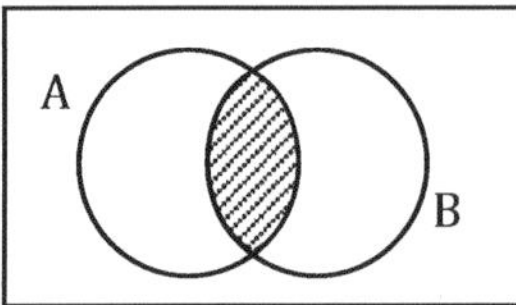

  For example: For $A = \{2, 3\}, B = \{1, 3, 5\}, A \cap B = \{3\}$

- **Difference of Two Sets:** Difference of two sets A and B, i.e. $A - B$ is a set of elements present in set A but not in set B.

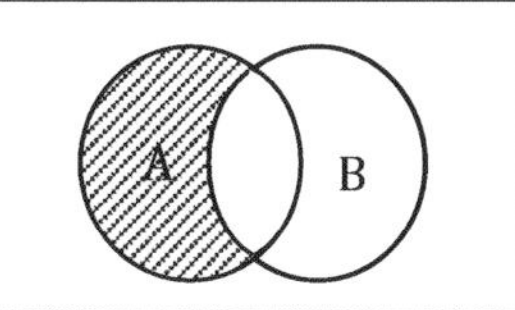

For example: For $A = \{2,\ 4\}$, $B = \{2,\ 6,\ 5\}$, $A - B = \{4\}$, $B - A = \{5,\ 6\}$

- **Complement:** Complement of set A, i.e. A^{-1} or A' is a set that contains the elements outside set A.

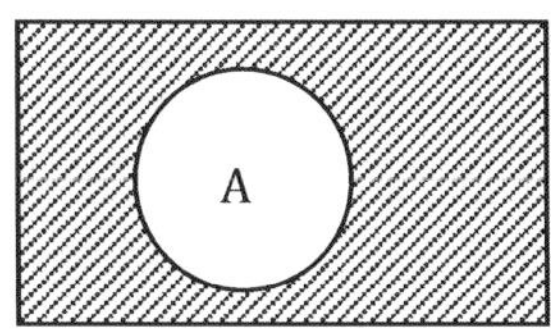

For example: If $A = \{1,\ 2\}$ and Universal Set U $= \{1,\ 2,\ 7,\ 8\}$, $A' = \{7,\ 8\}$

A few important rules:

- For two sets A and B:
  - $A \cup B = A + B - A \cap B \ldots$(i)
  - $(A \cup B)' = A' \cap B' \ldots$(ii)
  - $(A \cap B)' = A' \cup B' \ldots$(iii)

  Let us see how:

  We refer to the diagram given below:

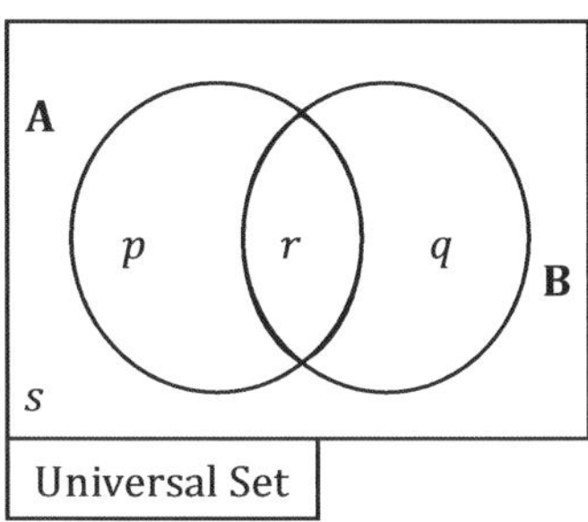

The cardinal numbers of the regions are shown as p, q, r and s.

We have:

$A = p + r$, $B = q + r$, $A \cap B = r$, $A \cup B = p + r + q$

Thus, we have:

$A \cup B = p + q + r = (p + r) + (q + r) - r$

$= A + B - A \cap B \ldots$(i)

$=> (A \cup B)' = s$

We also have: $A' = q + s,\ B' = p + s => A' \cap B' = s$

$=> (A \cup B)' = A' \cap B' \ldots$(ii)

Similarly:

$(A \cap B)' = p + q + s$

Also, $A' \cup B' = A' + B' - A' \cap B' = (q + s) + (p + s) - s = p + q + s$

$=> (A \cap B)' = A' \cup B' \ldots$(iii)

- For three sets A, B and C:

  $A \cup B \cup C = A + B + C - (A \cap B + B \cap C + C \cap A) + A \cap B \cap C$

  Let us see how:

  The cardinal numbers of the regions are shown:

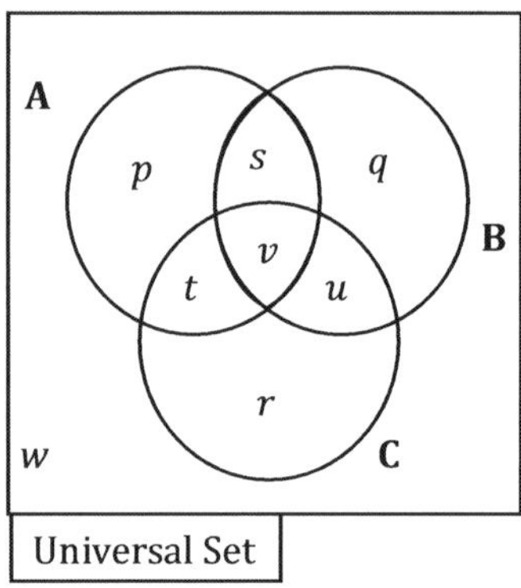

$A = p + s + t + v$

$B = q + s + u + v$

$C = r + t + u + v$

$A \cap B = s + v,\ A \cap C = t + v,\ B \cap C = u + v$

$A \cap B \cap C = v$

$A \cup B \cup C = p + q + r + s + t + u + v$

Also, $A \cap B + B \cap C + C \cap A = (s + v) + (t + v) + (u + v) = s + t + u + 3v$

$=> A + B + C - (A \cap B + B \cap C + C \cap A) + A \cap B \cap C$

$= (p + s + t + v) + (q + s + u + v) + (r + t + u + v) - (s + t + u + 3v) + v$

$= p + q + r + s + t + u + v$

$= A \cup B \cup C$

Let us take a few examples:

(1) In a survey, it was found that 65 people keep dogs as pets, 70 people keep cats, 40 people keep birds, 20 people keep both dogs and cats, 10 people keep both cats and birds, 5 people keep both birds and dogs and 3 people keep all three. How many people participated in the survey if it is known that each person has at least one pet?

Explanation:

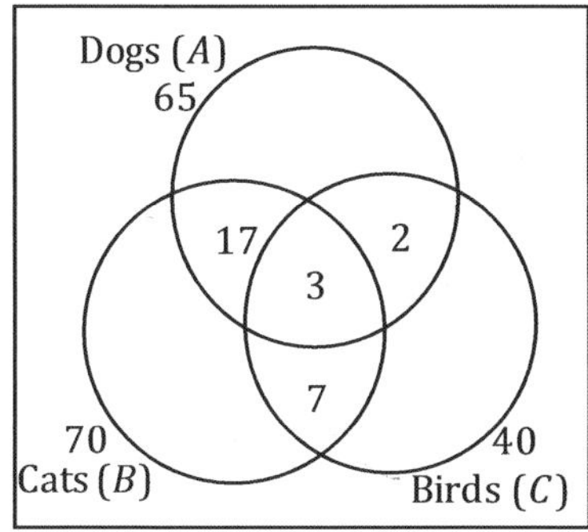

$A = 65,\ B = 40,\ C = 70$

$A \cap B = 20,\ B \cap C = 10,\ C \cap A = 5$

$A \cap B \cap C = 3$

The total number of people surveyed

$= A \cup B \cup C$

$= A + B + C - (A \cap B + B \cap C + C \cap A) + A \cap B \cap C$

$= 65 + 40 + 70 - (20 + 10 + 5) + 3 = 143$

(2) In a class of 50 boys, some play cricket, some football and some hockey. The number of boys who play cricket is more than those who play football, which is more than those who play hockey, which is more than those who play only two games, which is more than those who play all three games. If each boy plays at least one game and there is at least one boy who plays all three games, what is the minimum number of boys who play football?

Explanation:

We know that the boys play cricket (C), football (F) or hockey (H).

As the information,

50 = C + F + H − Only two games + All three games

In order to minimize F, we need to minimize the number of students in the regions a, b, c and d, as shown in the diagram below.

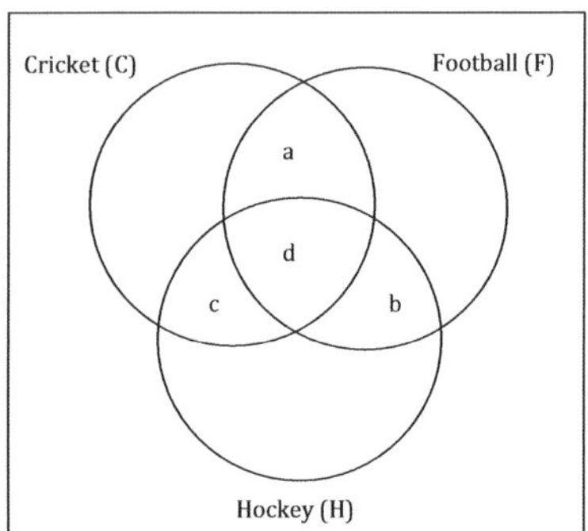

$50 = \text{C} + \text{F} + \text{H} - (a + b + c) + d$

Since $C > F > H >$ (a + b + c) $> d \geq 1$, we assume d = 1, a + b + c = 2, and H = 3.

This follows that F = 4 (minimum)

So, we make the following distribution:

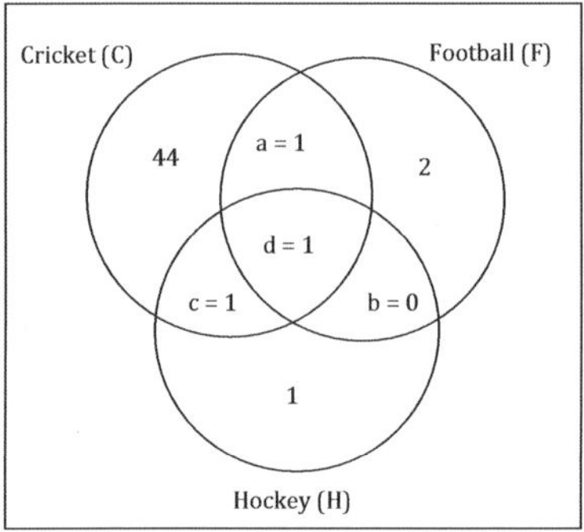

We have: C = 50 − 4 − 3 − 2 − 1 = 44, F = 4, H = 3, a = 1, b = 0, c = 1, and d = 1.

2.2 Statistics

Statistics is the study of the collection, analysis and interpretation of data. Some of the most commonly used statistical measures are the Mean, Median, Range, and Standard Deviation.

Let us discuss them.

Arithmetic mean:

- For a set of n numbers $x_1, x_2, x_3, \ldots x_n$, the arithmetic mean is calculated as:

$$\overline{x} = \frac{\text{Sum of the } n \text{ numbers}}{n} = \frac{x_1 + x_2 + x_3 + \cdots + x_n}{n}$$

- If $x_1, x_2, x_3, \ldots x_n$ be n observations and $f_1, f_2, f_3, \ldots f_n$, be their corresponding frequencies, their arithmetic mean is calculated as:

$$\overline{x} = \frac{x_1 \times f_1 + x_2 \times f_2 + \ldots x_n \times f_n}{f_1 + f_2 + \cdots + f_n}$$

For ease of calculations, the mean can be calculated easily using the method of 'deviation about the mean', as shown below:

Let the assumed mean be x_a

The observations are modified by subtracting x_a from each of the values as follows:

$x_1 \equiv x_1 - x_a$

$x_2 \equiv x_2 - x_a$

...

...

$x_n \equiv x_n - x_a$

The means are now calculated as shown:

- For a set of n numbers $x_1, x_2, x_3, \ldots x_n$, the arithmetic mean is calculated as:

$$\overline{x} = x_a + \frac{(x_1 - x_a) + (x_2 - x_a) + (x_3 - x_a) + \cdots + (x_n - x_a)}{n}$$

- If $x_1, x_2, x_3, \ldots x_n$ be n observations and $f_1, f_2, f_3, \ldots f_n$, be their corresponding frequencies, their arithmetic mean is calculated as:

$$\overline{x} = x_a + \frac{(x_1 - x_a) \times f_1 + (x_2 - x_a) \times f_2 + \ldots (x_n - x_a) \times f_n}{f_1 + f_2 + \cdots + f_n}$$

Let us take a few examples:

(1) What is the mean of 123, 134, 128, 139, 141, and 127?

Explanation:

$$\text{Mean} = \frac{123 + 134 + 128 + 139 + 141 + 127}{6} = 132$$

Alternate Approach:

Let the assumed mean = 134.

Thus, the deviations are:

- $123 - 134 = -11$
- $134 - 134 = 0$
- $128 - 134 = -6$
- $139 - 134 = 5$
- $141 - 134 = 7$
- $127 - 134 = -7$

$$\Rightarrow \text{Mean} = 134 + \frac{-11 + 0 - 6 + 5 + 7 - 7}{6} = 134 - \frac{12}{6} = 132$$

(2) What is the mean of the observations shown below?

Observations	Frequencies
11	14
7	8
15	6
13	12

Explanation:

We have:

Observations	Frequencies	Observation × Frequency
11	14	$11 \times 14 = 154$
7	8	$7 \times 8 = 56$
15	6	$15 \times 6 = 90$
13	12	$13 \times 12 = 156$
	Total = 40	**Total = 154 + 56 + 90 + 156 = 456**

$$\Rightarrow \text{Mean} = \frac{456}{40} = 11.4$$

Alternate Approach:

Let the assumed mean be 11.

Thus, we have:

Observations	Modified Observation = Observation − Assumed mean	Freq.	Mod. Obs. × Freq.
11	11 − 11 = 0	14	0 × 14 = 0
7	7 − 11 = − 4	8	(− 4) × 8 = − 32
15	15 − 11 = 4	6	4 × 6 = 24
13	13 − 11 = 2	12	2 × 12 = 24
		Total = 40	**Total = 16**

$=> \text{Mean} = 11 + \frac{16}{40} = 11.4$

Median:

Median refers to the middle value of all observations arranged in ascending or descending order.

Thus, we have:

- **If n is odd:** Median = Value of the $\left(\frac{n+1}{2}\right)^{\text{th}}$ observation.
- **If n is even:** Median = Average of $\left(\frac{n}{2}\right)^{\text{th}}$ and $\left(\frac{n}{2}+1\right)^{\text{th}}$ observations.

Let us take a few examples:

(1) What is the median of 123, 134, 128, 139, 141 and 126 ?

Explanation:

After arranging data in ascending order, we have:

123, 126, 128, 134, 139, 141

Since there are 6 (even) terms, we have:

$$\text{Median} = \frac{\left(\frac{6}{2}\right)^{\text{th}} \text{term} + \left(\frac{6}{2}+1\right)^{\text{th}} \text{term}}{2} = \frac{3^{\text{rd}} \text{term} + 4^{\text{th}} \text{term}}{2}$$

123, 126, $\underset{3^{\text{rd}}}{\underline{128}}$, $\underset{4^{\text{th}}}{\underline{134}}$, 139, 141

$= \frac{128+134}{2} = 131$

(2) What is the median of the observations shown below?

Observations	Frequencies
11	12
7	8
15	6
13	14

Explanation:

After arranging the observations in ascending order, we have:

Observations	Frequencies	Cumulative Frequency
7	8	8
11	12	12 + 8 = 20
13	14	14 + 20 = 34
15	6	6 + 34 = 40
	Total = 40	

Since there are 40 observations, we have:

$$\text{Median} = \frac{\left(\frac{40}{2}\right)^{\text{th}} \text{term} + \left(\frac{40}{2} + 1\right)^{\text{th}} \text{term}}{2} = \frac{20^{\text{th}}\ \text{term} + 21^{\text{st}}\ \text{term}}{2}$$

Observations	Frequencies	Cumulative Frequency	
7	8	8	
11 <—	12	12 + 8 = 20 <—	**20th term**
13 <—	14	14 + 20 = 34 <—	**21st term**
15	6	6 + 34 = 40	
	Total = 40		

$$\text{Median} = \frac{11 + 13}{2} = 12$$

Range:

Range refers to the difference between the values of maximum and minimum observations.

For example, the range of the set of observations 11, 13, 23, 21, 13, 17, 19 is 23 − 11 = 12

Standard Deviation:

Standard deviation shows the spread of the observations. If the observations are far away from the mean, the standard deviation would be high; similarly, if the observations are close to the mean, the standard deviation would be low.

For a set of n numbers $x_1, x_2, x_3, \ldots x_n$, the Standard Deviation (s) is calculated as:

If $\overline{x}$ is the mean of the observations:

$$s = \sqrt{\frac{(x_1 - \overline{x})^2 + (x_2 - \overline{x})^2 + \cdots + (x_n - \overline{x})^2}{n}}$$

Let us take an example:

(1) What is the standard deviation of 12, 15, 16 and 17 ?

$$\text{Mean} = \overline{x} = \frac{12 + 15 + 16 + 17}{4} = 15$$

$$=> s = \sqrt{\frac{(12 - 15)^2 + (15 - 15)^2 + (16 - 15)^2 + (17 - 15)^2}{4}}$$

$$= \sqrt{\frac{9 + 0 + 1 + 4}{4}} = \sqrt{3.5} = 1.87$$

A few important rules:

For a set of n numbers: $x_1, x_2, x_3, \ldots x_n$

- If a constant number k is added to (or subtracted from) each term of the above set of observations, we have:
  - The Mean increases (or decreases) by k
  - The Median increases (or decreases) by k
  - The Range remains unchanged
  - The Standard Deviation remains unchanged

- If a constant number k is multiplied (divided) to each term of the above set of observations, we have:
  - The Mean is multiplied (divided) by k
  - The Median is multiplied (divided) by k
  - The Range is multiplied (divided) by k
  - The Standard Deviation is multiplied (divided) by k

- If a new term, whose value is equal to the mean, is introduced in the above set of observations, we have:
  - The Mean remains unchanged
  - Nothing can be concluded about Median; it depends on the distribution
  - The Range remains unchanged
  - The Standard Deviation decreases

- If the terms of a set of observations arranged in ascending or descending order have a constant difference between consecutive terms, i.e., they form an Arithmetic Sequence, we have: Mean = Median

2.3 Data Interpretation

Data Interpretation mainly involves questions based on tables, charts, line graphs, bar graphs, pie charts, etc. The data has to be assimilated and used to answer the questions that follow. A single question can have multiple data forms. Thus, one may need to read the data quickly, compare them and draw conclusions.

This is not simply a test of speedy calculation. One has to be able to derive logical inferences from the data simultaneously, doing quick calculations.

In order to do calculations, one should be aware of calculation short-cut methods. The most important calculation involves division and calculating the percentage, which takes up a lot of time if done using conventional methods. Thus, the knowledge of short-cut division methods and ratio comparison methods are very handy.

Fraction calculations

Comparing fractions: Different methods exist for comparing fractions. The methods are given below:

- Of two fractions, if their denominators are equal, the fraction with the greatest numerator is the greatest.
- Of two fractions, if their numerators are equal, the fraction with the smallest denominator is the greatest.
- Of two fractions, if one fraction has greater numerator and smaller denominator, it is the greater one.
    - For example: Between $\frac{5}{13}$ and $\frac{9}{11}$, the latter is the greater fraction.
- For fractions less than 1, if the difference between the numerator and its denominator is equal for all the fractions, the fraction with the greatest numerator is the greatest.
    - For example: Among $\frac{2}{3}, \frac{5}{6}, \frac{9}{10}$, and $\frac{11}{12}$, the last fraction $\frac{11}{12}$ is the greatest.
- For fractions greater than 1, if the difference between the numerator and its denominator is equal for all the fractions, the fraction with the least numerator is the greatest.
    - For example: Among $\frac{3}{2}, \frac{6}{5}, \frac{10}{9}$, and $\frac{12}{11}$, the first fraction $\frac{3}{2}$ is the greatest.
- We can compare fractions by making the numerator equal to '1' for all fractions and calculating approximate value of the denominator of each fraction.
    - For example: For the fractions $\frac{5}{13}$ and $\frac{9}{20}$, we make the numerator 1 for both.
      This gives us: $\frac{5}{13} = \frac{5/5}{13/5} = \frac{1}{2.6}$ and $\frac{9}{20} = \frac{9/9}{20/9} = \frac{1}{2.2}$

Since the latter $\left(\frac{9}{20}\right)$ has a smaller denominator, it is a greater fraction.

- Yet another method of comparing fractions is to cross-multiply the numerator of one fraction and the denominator of the other fraction and then compare the products.

  - For example: For the fractions $\frac{13}{23}$ and $\frac{7}{13}$

    We multiply 13 and 13 to get 169 and on the other hand multiply 7 and 23 to get 161.

    Since 169 > 161, we have: $13 \times 13 > 7 \times 23 => \frac{13}{23} > \frac{7}{13}$.

Different ways of representing data:

Let us discuss the data given in a tabular form:

The following table gives the production of different electronic goods (in thousands) by a company 'X' in the years 2013 and 2014:

A table:

Item	2013	2014
TVs	120	180
Laptops	240	270
Hard Disks	100	130
DVDs	140	120
Mobiles	200	300

The same data can be represented in different forms as shown below:

A pie chart:

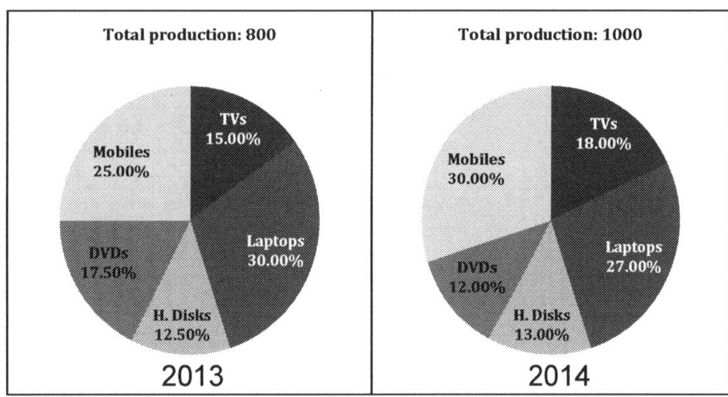

The same data can be represented in the form of a bar graph as shown below:

A bar graph:

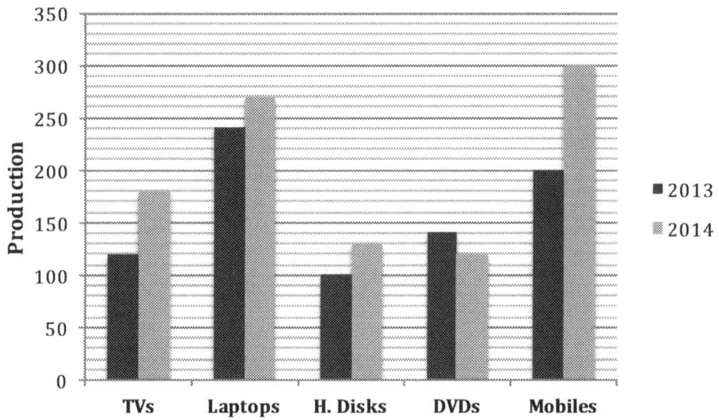

A stacked bar graph:

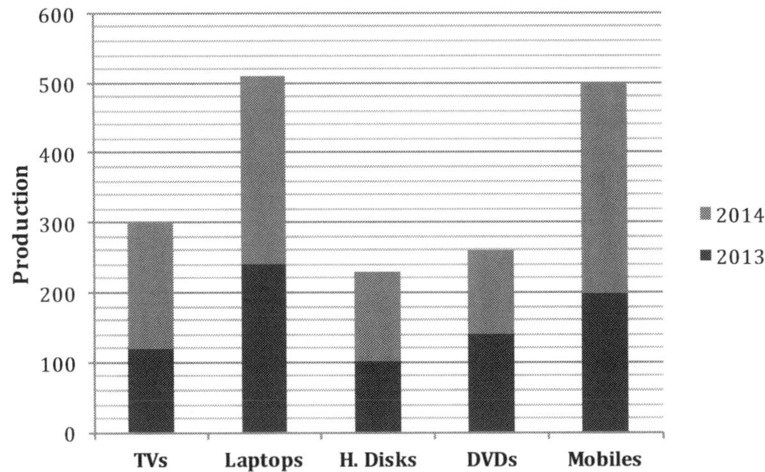

A horizontal bar graph:

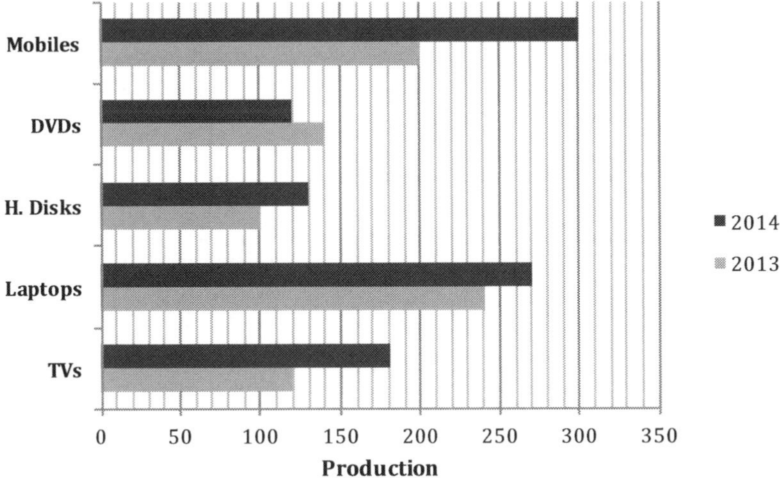

A line graph:

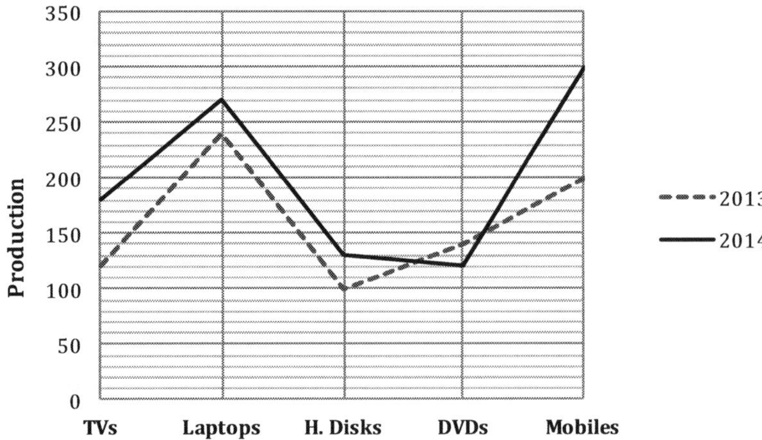

A scatter plot:

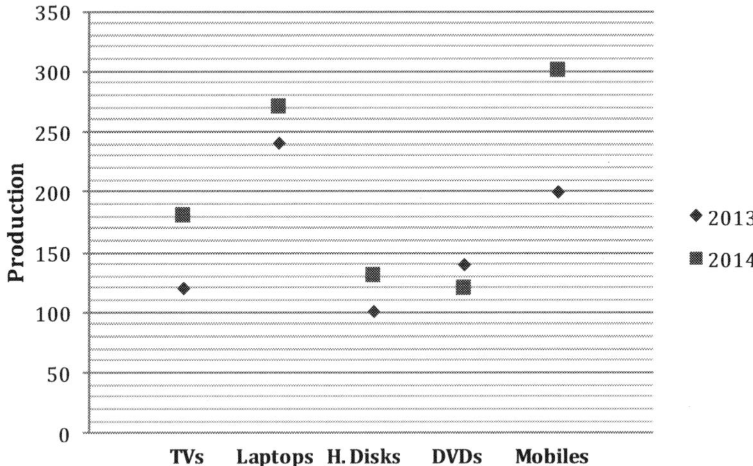

Few questions based on the above graphs:

- **Table:**

  What is the percentage change in the production of TVs from 2013 to 2014?

  Explanation:

  Percentage change

  $$= \frac{\text{Final value} - \text{Initial value}}{\text{Initial value}} \times 100 = \frac{180 - 120}{120} \times 100$$

  $$= \frac{60}{120} \times 100 = 50\%$$

- **Table:**

  What is the average production value of all electronic items (in thousands) in 2013?

  Explanation:

  Here, we simply need to take the average of all the production values in the year 2013.

  $$\text{Average} = \frac{120 + 240 + 100 + 140 + 200}{5} = \frac{800}{5} = 160.$$

- **Bar graph:**

  Which item has the smallest percentage increase in its production from 2013 to 2014?

  Explanation:

  Here we need to compare the percentage changes for each item and select the minimum value.

  For minimum % change, the initial base value should be high and the corresponding change should be low.

  We see that Laptops have a high initial value and the change is also small, so Laptops could be a possible answer. Among the others, DVDs have a decrease, so cannot be the answer, while the others have a relatively large change in their values.

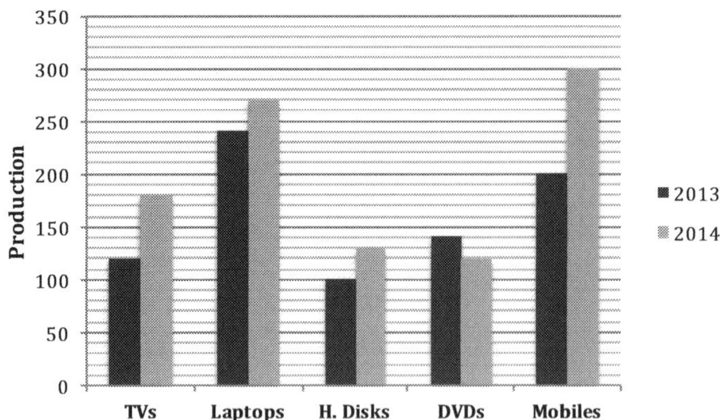

Thus, the answer is 'Laptops,'

Listing down the actual % changes for each item, we have:

Item	2013	2014	% change
TVs	120	180	50.0
Laptops	240	270	12.5
Hard Disks	100	130	30.0
DVDs	140	120	– 14.3
Mobiles	200	300	50.0

Thus, it is clear that the answer we obtained by reasoning is correct. Hence, we have arrived at the correct answer without doing a single calculation.

- **Bar graph:**

What is the net difference in total production (in thousands) between 2013 and 2014?

Explanation:

We can simply add up the values of 2013 and 2014 and subtract them.

Alternately, we can find the difference between each food item in each year and add up the differences (with sign):

Item	2013	2014	Difference
TVs	120	180	+60
Laptops	240	270	+30
Hard Disks	100	130	+30
DVDs	140	120	– 20
Mobiles	200	300	+100
Net difference			**200**

- **Line graph:**

What is the maximum percentage change in production of any item from 2013 to 2014 ?

Explanation:

For this, we first need to identify which item has the maximum % change.

Looking at the line graph, it is clear that the item may be mobiles or TVs, since each has a large difference in its two-year values.

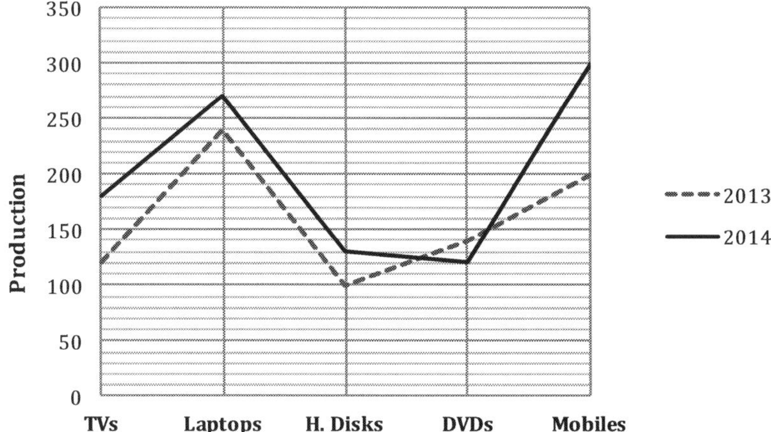

Percent increase in TVs

$$= \frac{180 - 120}{120} \times 100 = 50\%$$

Percent increase in Mobiles

$$= \frac{300 - 200}{200} \times 100 = 50\%$$

Thus, the answer is 50%.

- **Pie chart:**

What is the angle subtended at the center by Laptops in 2013?

Explanation:

We need to convert the % values given in the pie chart to degrees.

We know that 100% corresponds to 360°.

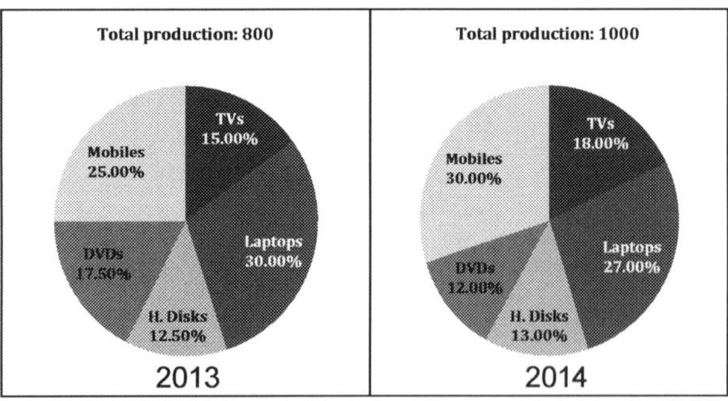

In 2013, Laptops are represented by 30% in the pie chart.

Thus, the corresponding degree measure

$$\frac{30}{100} \times 360° = 108°$$

- **Pie chart:**

What is the percentage change in production of TVs from 2013 to 2014?

Explanation:

We need to understand that in the first pie chart, share of TVs is 15% of 800, while in the second pie chart, it is 18% of 1000.

Thus, number of TVs in 2013 = $\frac{15}{100} \times 800 = 120$

The number of TVs in 2014 = $\frac{18}{100} \times 1000 = 180$

Thus, required percent change

$$= \frac{180 - 120}{120} \times 100 = 50\%$$

- **Pie chart:**

Compared to 2013, in 2014, production of which items has decreased?

Explanation:

We see that the total production, taking all the items, has increased from 2013 to 2014.

Hence, the items whose % values have gone up from 2013 to 2014 would imply an increase in production.

Only those items whose % values have decreased would possibly have decreased production values.

Thus, possible items are Laptops (decreased from 30% to 27.5%) and DVDs (decreased from 17.5% to 12%).

Laptops:

The number of Laptops in 2013 = $\frac{30}{100} \times 800 = 240$

The number of Laptops in 2014 = $\frac{27}{100} \times 1000 = 270$

Thus, the number of Laptops has rather increased.

DVDs:

The number of DVDs in 2013 = $\frac{17.5}{100} \times 800 = 140$

The number of DVDs in 2014 = $\frac{12}{100} \times 1000 = 120$

Thus, only DVDs' production has decreased.

- **Pie chart:**

If it was found that the production of TVs has been under-reported by 40% in 2013, what is actual percentage share of TVs in 2013?

Explanation:

Assuming the total production as 100 units, production of TVs 15% of 100 = 15 units.

Since TVs have been under-reported by 40%, we can say that 15 units correspond to 100% − 40% = 60% of the actual production of TVs.

Hence actual production of TVs

$\frac{15}{60} \times 100 = 25$

Thus, the number of TVs have increased in value by 25 − 15 = 10 units

Thus, the total would also increase by 10 units and would become 110 units

Thus, actual percentage share of TVs

$$= \frac{25}{110} \times 100 = \frac{250}{11}\% = 22\frac{8}{11}\%$$

- **Pie chart:**

If it was found that the production of Laptops has been under-reported by 20% in 2013, which of the following options can represent the actual % share of any items in 2013?

(A) 3.3%
(B) 23.3%
(C) 28.2%
(D) 41.5%

Explanation:

Since the production of Laptops has been under-reported, its actual % share is going to increase and hence, the % share of the other items would decrease.

Assuming the total production equal to 100 units, production of Laptops = 30% of 100 = 30 units

Since Laptops have been under-reported by 20%, we can say that 30 units correspond to 80% of the actual production.

Hence actual production of Laptops $= \frac{30}{80} \times 100 = 37.5$ units

Thus, Laptops have increased in value by $37.5 - 30 = 7.5$ units

Thus, the total would also increase by 7.5 units and would become 107.5 units.

Since the increase in the total is only slight, the % share of Laptops would increase and that of the others would decrease only by a very slight amount.

Thus, the only possible % could be 23.3% $\left(= \frac{25}{107.5} \times 100\%\right)$, that of Mobiles, when it reduces from 25%.

- **Pie chart:**

If the % distribution of production of the items is the same in the year 2015 as it is in 2014, while the total production increases by 20% from that in 2014, what would be the production value of Mobiles in 2015?

Explanation:

Total production in 2015 = 1000 + 20% of 1000 = 1200

Since the % distribution of the items remains the same, production of Mobiles

$= 30\% \text{ of } 1200 = \frac{30}{100} \times 1200 = 360$

- **Scatter plot:**

If, in 2014, the ratio of the selling price of a Mobile to the selling price of a Laptop is 1 : 2, what is the ratio of the sales proceeds of Mobiles to the sales proceeds of Laptops in 2014?

Explanation:

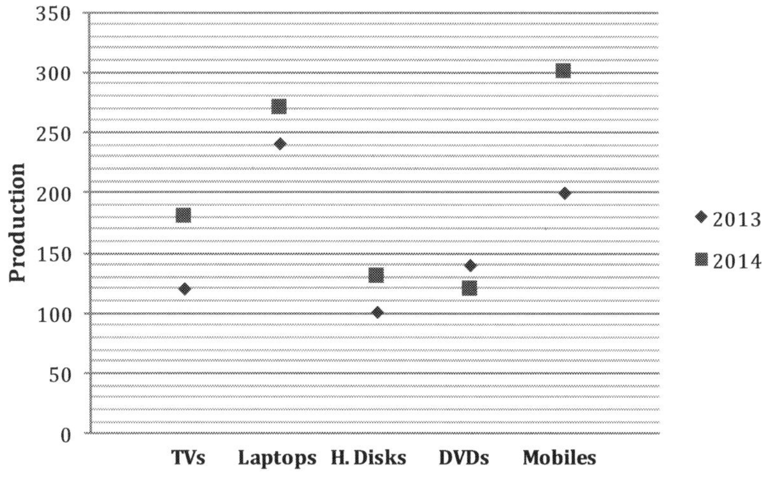

Production of Mobiles in 2014 = 300

Production of Laptops in 2014 = 270

Thus, ratio of production of Mobiles to that of Laptops

$= \frac{300}{270} = \frac{10}{9}$

Ratio of the selling price of a Mobile to the selling price of a Laptop $= \frac{1}{2}$

Hence, ratio of the sales proceeds of Mobiles to the sales proceeds of Laptops

$= \frac{10}{9} \times \frac{1}{2} = \frac{5}{9}$

- **Scatter plot:**

If the % change in production of Hard Disks from 2014 to 2015 is the same as that in the 2013 to 2014 and the production of Hard Disks represents 10% of the total production in 2015, what is the total production (in thousands) of all items in 2015?

Explanation:

We know that

Hard Disks production in 2013 = 100

Hard Disks production in 2014 = 130

Thus, % change in Hard Disks production from 2013 to 2014

$$\frac{130 - 100}{100} \times 100 = 30\%$$

Since the % increase in 2015 remains the same, the production of Hard Disks in 2015

$= 130 + 30\%$ of $130 = 130 + 39 = 169$

Since this represents 10% of total production in 2015, total production

$$= \frac{169}{10} \times 100 = 1690$$

In the next chapter, you will find 100 exam-like questions. Best of luck!

Chapter 3

Practice Questions

3.1 Multiple Choice Questions

1. There are a total of 66 students in a school. They have to study at least one of three subjects – Mathematics, Physics and Economics. Out of these, 28 students did not choose either Physics or Economics; 15 students did not choose either Mathematics or Economics; 45 students did not choose Economics; and 30 students did not choose Mathematics. The number of students who did not choose either Mathematics or Economics exceeded the number of students who did not choose Mathematics or Physics by 2. If 5 students chose all three subjects, how many students chose both Economics and Mathematics?

   (A) 1

   (B) 5

   (C) 6

   (D) 7

   (E) 10

   Solve yourself:

2. In a survey of 63 people, 33 people subscribed to magazine A, 30 people subscribed to magazine B and 17 subscribed to magazine C. For any two of the magazines, 9 people subscribed to both the magazines. If 5 people in the survey did not subscribe to any of the three magazines, how many people subscribed to all three magazines?

   (A) 10

   (B) 9

   (C) 7

   (D) 5

   (E) 2

   Solve yourself:

3. Out of 38 students in a class, 10 students like baseball, 20 students like football and 10 students like rugby. One student likes only baseball and football, 2 students like only football and rugby, and 4 students like only baseball and rugby. If only 2 students like all three games, how many students do not like any of the above three games?

   (A) 3

   (B) 5

(C) 6

(D) 9

(E) 11

Solve yourself:

4. In a class, 5 students failed in all three subjects: Biology, Physics and History; 13 students failed in at least two of the above mentioned subjects and 24 students failed in at least one of the above subjects. What is the difference between the number of students who passed in exactly two subjects and those who passed in exactly one subject?

(A) 3

(B) 5

(C) 8

(D) 11

(E) 13

Solve yourself:

5. Among 40 employees in an office, 33.33% of the men play rugby and 50% of the employees who play rugby are men. If 25% of the employees are women, how many employees are women who do not play rugby?

(A) 0

(B) 10

(C) 15

(D) 20

(E) 30

Solve yourself:

6. Out of 50 students in a class, 30 like dancing, 20 do not like singing and 10 like only dancing. How many students do not like dancing but like singing?

(A) 5

(B) 10

(C) 15

(D) 20

(E) 30

Solve yourself:

7. John, a student of the ninth grade with a total of 50 students, scored 75 in an exam in which the mean score of all students was 70 and standard deviation of the scores was 2. Bob, a student of the tenth grade with a total of 50 students, scored 72 in an exam in which the mean score of all students was 65 and standard deviation of the scores was 3. Which of the following statements must be correct?

I. John ranks higher in his class than Bob does in his class.

II. There was at least one student who scored more than John.

III. There was at least one student who scored less than Bob.

(A) Only I

(B) Only II

(C) Only III

(D) Only I and III

(E) Only II and III

Solve yourself:

8. The average (arithmetic mean) of five positive integers k, m, r, s and t is 16, and $k < m < r < s < t$. If t is 40, what is the greatest possible value of the median of the five integers?

(A) 16

(B) 18

(C) 19

(D) 20

(E) 38

Solve yourself:

9.

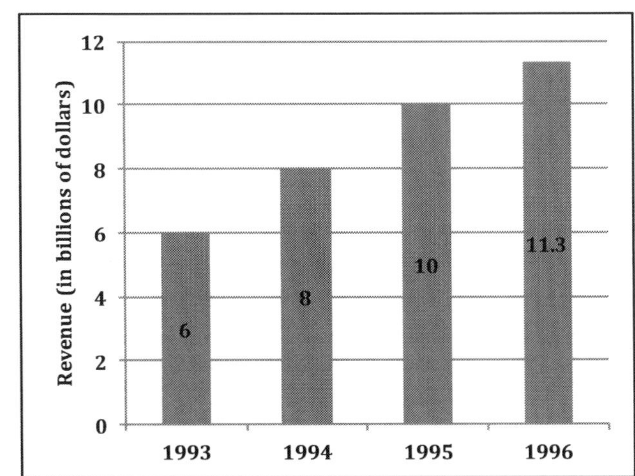

The graph above shows the combined revenue, in billions of dollars, of a chain of food stores for a four-year period. In 1994 a certain store's revenue accounted for 2.0 percent of the combined revenue for that year, and in 1995 the same store accounted for 2.3 percent of the combined revenue for that year. What was the approximate percent increase in revenue for this store from 1994 to 1995?

(A) 0.3%

(B) 15.0%

(C) 25.0%

(D) 30.4%

(E) 43.8%

Solve yourself:

10. A student scored 43, 47, 39, 27, and 34 in five tests he took. What could be the score in his sixth test, if after the sixth test, his mean score is equal to his median score?

I. 29

II. 36

III. 56

(A) Only I

(B) Only II

(C) Only III

(D) Only I and III

(E) I, II and III

Solve yourself:

11.

Car Brand	Sales
A	500
B	350
C	160
D	320
E	120
Total	**1450**

The table above gives the sales in City X for five car brands. If the total sales of these car brands was 30 percent of the city's total sales, the sales of car brand D was what percent of the sale of the car brands that are not part of the above table?

(A) 8.57%

(B) 12.44%

(C) 16.67%

(D) 20.0%

(E) 25.0%

Solve yourself:

12. A man compared the cost of two brands of gasoline for his car, driving it at 40 miles per hour speed. The gasoline costs and consumption rates for Speedex brand of gasoline are \$2.50 and 50 miles per gallon, respectively, and those for Zoomex brand of gasoline are \$2.20 and 33 miles per gallon, respectively. How many more miles can his car be driven at 40 miles per hour speed on \$50 worth of Speedex brand of gasoline than on \$50 worth of Zoomex brand of gasoline?

(A) 200

(B) 250

(C) 264

(D) 300

(E) 333

Solve yourself:

13.

Brand	Sales, 2015	Percent change from 2014
X	96	−20%
Y	246	−18%
Z	288	+20%
P	480	+200%
Q	100	+25%

The table above represents the sales figure of five car brands for the year 2015 in City X. Which brand had the greatest sales during the year 2014?

(A) X

(B) Y

(C) Z

(D) P

(E) Q

Solve yourself:

14.

Month	Number of cars sold
January	13
February	18
March	27
April	16

The table above shows the number of cars sold in each of four months this year. If the number of sales interactions made each month was proportional to the number of cars sold in that month, and if a total of 222 sales interactions were made in the four months shown, how many sales interactions were made in April?

(A) 39

(B) 40

(C) 42

(D) 48

(E) 54

Solve yourself:

15.

Number of defects	Number of batches
Less than 5	18
5 - 9	17
10 - 14	23
15 - 19	8
20 - 24	9
25 - 29	6
30 and above	2

A company manufactures AAA size batteries in batches. Last month it produced 81 batches of the batteries. The table above shows the distribution of number of batches according to the number of defects a batch of the batteries has. As per the information, if D is the median number of defects of the 81 batches, then D must satisfy which of the following?

(A) $5 \leq D \leq 9$

(B) $10 \leq D \leq 14$

(C) $15 \leq D \leq 19$

(D) $20 \leq D \leq 24$

(E) $25 \leq D \leq 29$

Solve yourself:

16. A set of 15 different integers has a median of 30 and a range of 30. What is the greatest possible integer that could be in this set?

(A) 42

(B) 47

(C) 50

(D) 53

(E) 60

Solve yourself:

17. The mean of the set of integers {4, 4, 5, 5, 6, x} is $\frac{x^2}{2}$. What is the range of the above set of integers?

(A) 1

(B) 2

(C) 3

(D) 4

(E) 5

Solve yourself:

18. A club has a total of x numbers of members, where x is an odd integer, and no two members have the same age. When the ages of the members are arranged in increasing order, the 21th age in the arrangement is the median age of the members. If the sum of the ages of the members is 1720, what is the average (arithmetic mean) of the ages of the club's members?

(A) 32

(B) 40

(C) 44

(D) 48

(E) 50

Solve yourself:

19. In a study it was observed that the number of microbes on Day 1 was 10 millions, while that on Day 3 increased to 14.4 millions. If the count of microbes increased by the same proportion during Day 1 to Day 2 and during Day 2 to Day 3 periods, how many microbes were there on Day 2?

(A) 12.0 millions

(B) 12.2 millions

(C) 12.5 millions

(D) 13.0 millions

(E) 13.5 millions

Solve yourself:

20. According to the table below, what was the approximate average sale value, in dollars, per bike sold on July 4 by a bicycle store?

Bikes sold by a store on July 4		
Type of bikes	Number of bikes sold	Price per bike (dollars)
52"	5	190
54"	7	210
56"	10	340
58"	12	360

(A) 161

(B) 194

(C) 233

(D) 297

(E) 348

Solve yourself:

21.

	2011 – 2012	
Attribute	**Bank X**	**Bank Y**
Loan Sanctions	650	1500
Total Revenue	1600	3500

The table above shows the performance of two banks, Bank X and Bank Y (all values are in million dollar) for the year 2011 – 2012. What is the positive difference between Loan Sanctions as a percent of Total Revenue for Bank X and that for Bank Y?

(A) 1.3

(B) 2.2

(C) 3.0

(D) 3.6

(E) 4.2

Solve yourself:

22.

Finances of company X		
Attribute	**2010**	**2011**
Total Income	250	450
Net Profit	125	150
Cash Profit	80	100

The above table shows the finances of Company X (all values are in million dollar) for the years 2010 and 2011. If the percent increase in Net Profits from 2010 to 2011 was the same as that from 2011 to 2012, while the Total Income of the company doubled from 2011 to 2012, what was the ratio of Net Profits to Total Income of the company in 2012?

(A) $\frac{1}{5}$

(B) $\frac{1}{4}$

(C) $\frac{1}{3}$

(D) $\frac{1}{2}$

(E) $\frac{4}{5}$

Solve yourself:

23. On Monday, 9 students took a test having 100 questions. The average (arithmetic mean) number of the correct answers was 50, and the median number of correct answers was 40. Which of the following statements must be true?

I. At least one student had more than 60 correct answers.

II. At least one student had more than 40 and less than 50 correct answers.

III. At least one student had less than 40 correct answers.

(A) Only I

(B) Only II

(C) Only III

(D) Only I and III

(E) Only II and III

Solve yourself:

24. The price per food item (in dollars) and the number of units of each item sold at Mac Mickey's on a particular day is shown in the line and the bar-graph below.

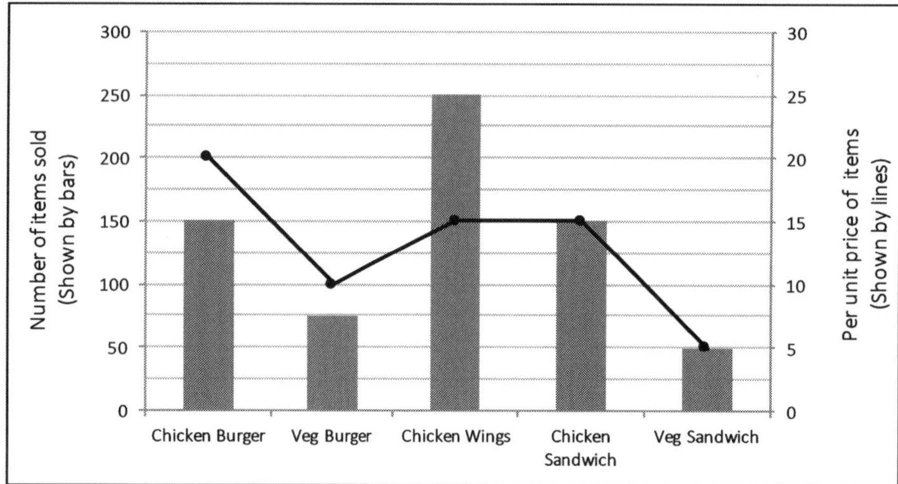

What is the median price of the food items sold on that day?

(A) \$10

(B) \$12

(C) \$14

(D) \$15

(E) \$16

Solve yourself:

The following three questions are based on the following bar chart.

The following graph shows the percent distribution of the number of employees of a company from 2010 to 2013 in four departments: R&D, HR, Sales and Finance.

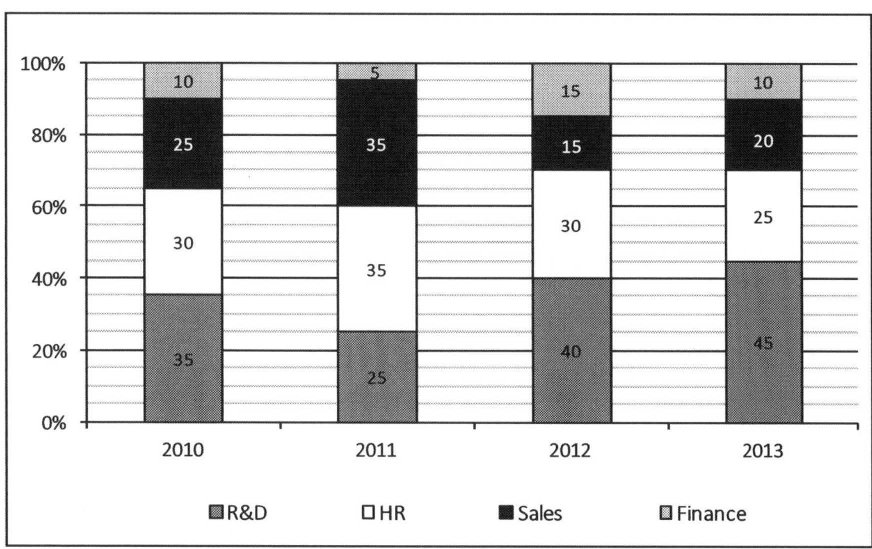

25. If the total number of employees remained the same throughout the years 2010 to 2013, what is the simple annual percent increase in the number of employees in R&D between 2010 and 2013?

(A) 2.50%

(B) 3.33%

(C) 7.15%

(D) 9.53%

(E) 10.00%

Solve yourself:

26. If the total strength of all employees in 2011 was 2500, and there was a 20% increase in total strength for every year from thereon, what is the number of employees in the Finance department in 2013?

(A) 300

(B) 350

(C) 360

(D) 432

(E) 450

Solve yourself:

27. If the total number of employees remained the same throughout the years 2010 to 2013, which department, and in which year, has the highest percent increase in the number of employees over the previous year?

 (A) Sales, 2011
 (B) HR, 2011
 (C) R&D, 2012
 (D) Finance, 2012
 (E) Sales, 2013

Solve yourself:

The following two questions are based on the following bar chart.

The graphs below show some information regarding the US-China trade from 2005-2010.

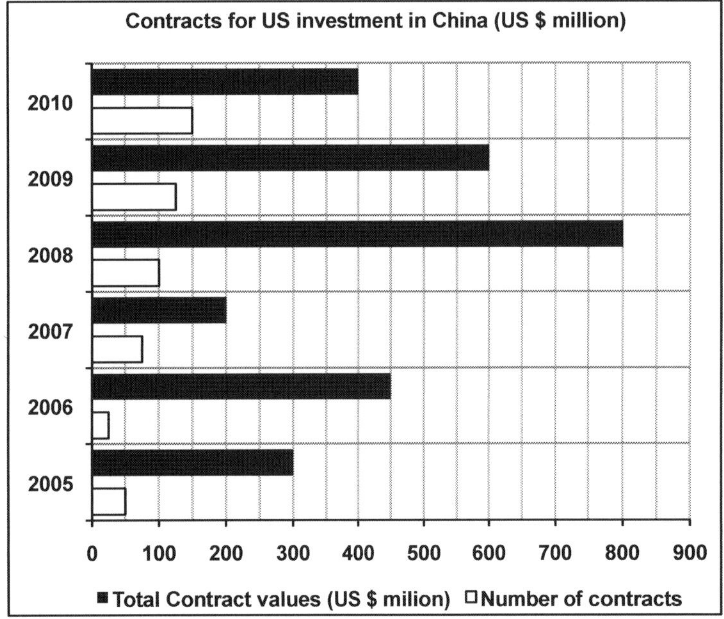

28. What is the percent change in the average value of a contract from 2005 to 2010?

(A) 66.7% decrease

(B) 55.5% decrease

(C) 11.1% increase

(D) 20.0% increase

(E) 33.3% increase

Solve yourself:

29. From the data provided, all of the following statements can be concluded EXCEPT:

(A) The number of contracts signed either increased or decreased in each year its previous year for the period 2005-2010.

(B) The total value of the contracts increased with increase in the number of contracts.

(C) The greatest increase in the number of contracts was in 2007 over 2006.

(D) In the period from 2005-2010 more than 500 contracts were signed for the US-China trade.

(E) Both A and B

Solve yourself:

The following four questions are based on the following bar chart.

The graph shows the exports of iron-ore from country X from January 2001 to December 2001.

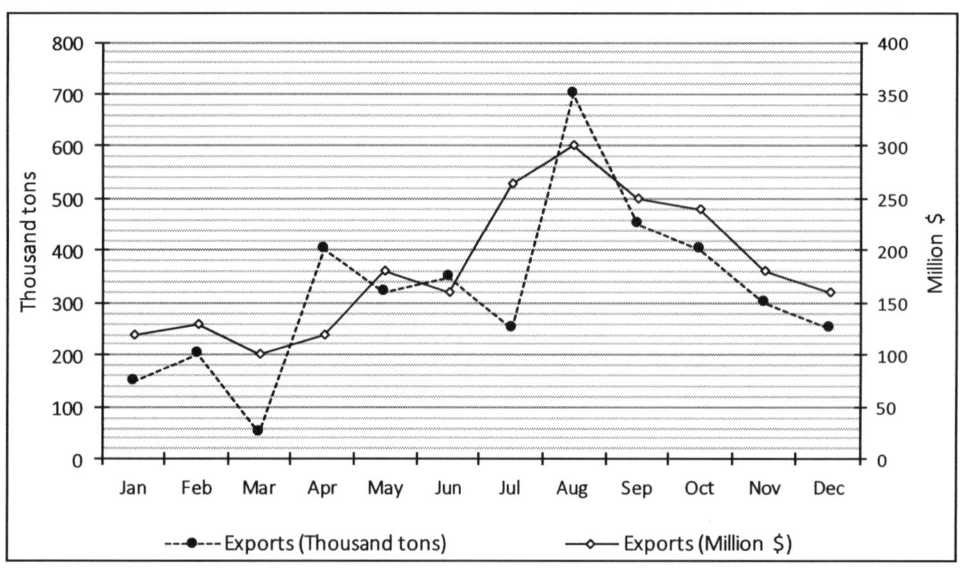

30. What is the average price, in dollars, per ton of iron-ore in December?

(A) \$6.15

(B) \$61.53

(C) \$615.38

(D) \$6153.80

(E) \$61538.00

Solve yourself:

31. In which of the FOLLOWING periods marks the maximum percentage decrease in the exports of iron-ore by volume (thousand tons) ?

(A) February - March

(B) April - May

(C) June - July

(D) August - September

(E) September - October

Solve yourself:

32. What was the approximate maximum price of iron-ore per ton in any of the months?

(A) \$600

(B) \$640

(C) \$800

(D) \$1060

(E) \$2000

Solve yourself:

33. What is the median volume of iron-ore exported (thousand tons) in the above period?

(A) 250

(B) 310

(C) 320

(D) 330

(E) 350

Solve yourself:

The following two questions are based on the following charts.

The graphs below show the profit (million dollars), revenue (million dollars) and the number of employees for XYZ Corporation for three years.

Expenditure in any year is calculated as the Revenue less the Profit.

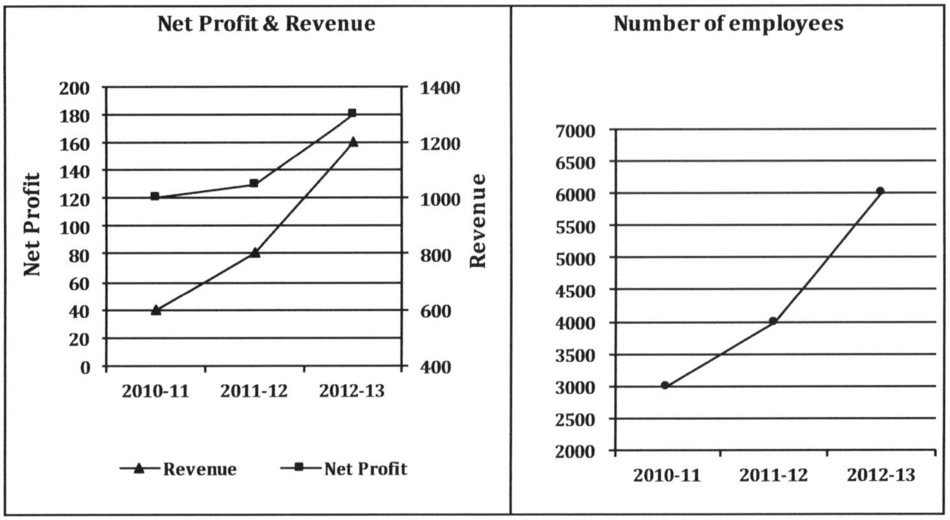

34. What is the percent increase in average expenditure per employee from 2010-11 to 2011-12?

(A) 2.8%

(B) 4.7%

(C) 5.3%

(D) 7.1%

(E) 8.2%

Solve yourself:

35. If the percent increase in the revenue from 2011-12 to 2012-13 is the same as that from 2012-13 to 2013-14, while the number of employees in 2013-14 remain the same as that in 2012-13, what is the average revenue, in million dollars, per employee in 2013-14?

(A) 0.15

(B) 0.24

(C) 0.30

(D) 0.42

(E) 0.75

Solve yourself:

The following two questions are based on the following chart.

The graph shows the sales and net profits of two companies, X and Y for four years. All figures are in billion dollars.

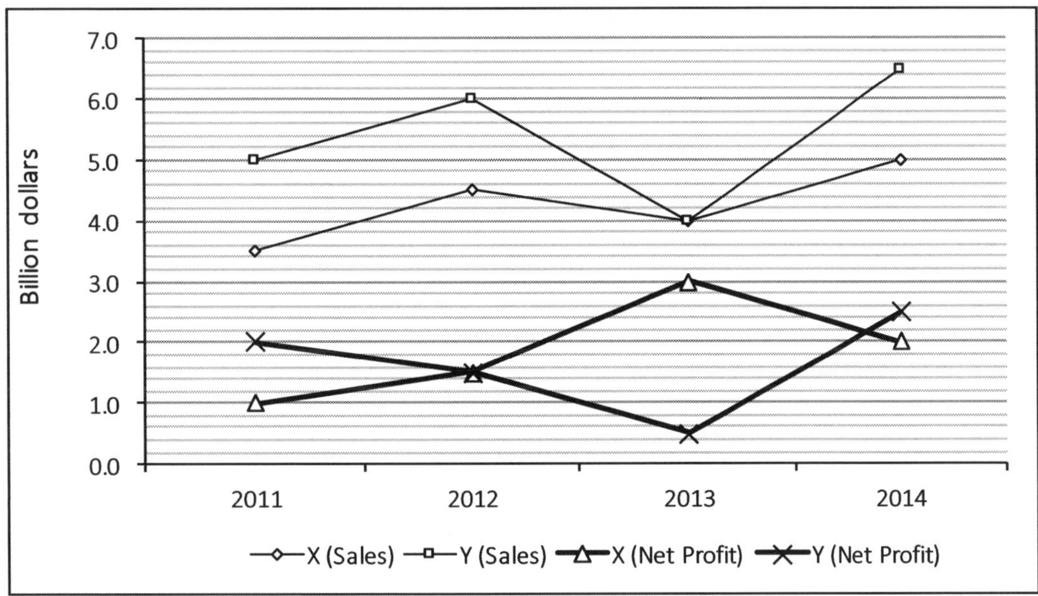

36. What was the highest ratio of net profit to sales for any year for Company X?

(A) 0.33

(B) 0.40

(C) 0.75

(D) 0.77

(E) 0.80

Solve yourself:

37. In which year(s), did the sales of Company X fall short of that of Company Y by more than 25%?

(A) 2011

(B) 2012

(C) 2013

(D) 2014

(E) Both in 2011 and 2014

Solve yourself:

38. The pie-chart shows the percent share of five-year revenue generated by Ola-cabs in India for the years 2011-2015. The total revenue generated in the five years is \$125 million.

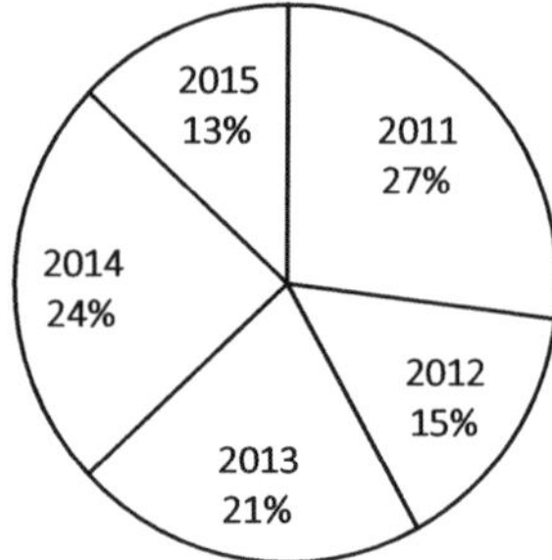

What is the difference, in million dollars, between the average revenue per year for five years and the revenue in the year closest to the average revenue per year?

(A) 0.50

(B) 1.00

(C) 1.25

(D) 1.50

(E) 2.00

Solve yourself:

The following three questions are based on the following chart.

Genre-wise percentage distribution of the Music-DVD market in Country X in 2010 is given in the pie-chart below. The Music-DVD market had a 60% share of the total music market, which was valued at $800 million.

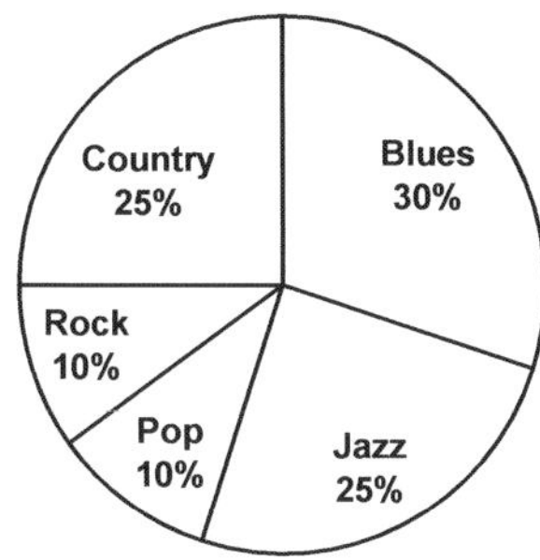

39. If Viacom-Music has 20% share in Music-DVD market and 5% share in the music markets other than Music-DVD market, what is the value, in million dollars, of Viacom-Music?

(A) 96
(B) 100
(C) 106
(D) 112
(E) 136

Solve yourself:

40. If the present Music-DVD market has grown by 20% over 2009 and the market for Jazz has grown by 50% over 2009, what was market share of Jazz in the Music-DVD market of 2009?

(A) 12.5%
(B) 20.0%
(C) 25.0%
(D) 30.0%
(E) 37.5%

Solve yourself:

41. The market for Blues in 2010 had been under-reported by 20% with all the other genres been reported correctly. If the error for Blues is corrected and a new pie-chart formed, what would be the approximate value of the correct percent share of Blues in the Music-DVD market in 2010?

(A) 25%

(B) 28%

(C) 30%

(D) 35%

(E) 40%

Solve yourself:

The following two questions are based on the following tabular information.

Three machines produce capacitors for electrical circuits. The capacitors are inspected and either accepted or rejected. The following table gives the number of capacitors rejected and the percentage of the total production accepted for each machine:

Machine no.	Number rejected	Percent of production accepted
P	250	75
Q	308	78
R	248	68

42. What is the total number of capacitors accepted as a percent of total capacitors produced by all three machines?

(A) 25.4%

(B) 34.0%

(C) 41.2%

(D) 73.7%

(E) 74.6%

Solve yourself:

43. For each defective circuit from Machine Q, a fine of \$0.50 has to be paid. What should be the cost for testing each capacitor from Machine Q so that one is indifferent to test the circuits?

(A) \$0.11

(B) \$0.32

(C) \$1.23

(D) \$1.87

(E) \$2.27

Solve yourself:

The following three questions are based on the following table and pie-charts.

The following table gives the number of families in a country in the years 2010 – 2013.

Year	No. of families (Millions)
2010	80
2011	85
2012	90
2013	95

The following charts give the distribution of families based on the number of members in a family for the years 2010 and 2013.

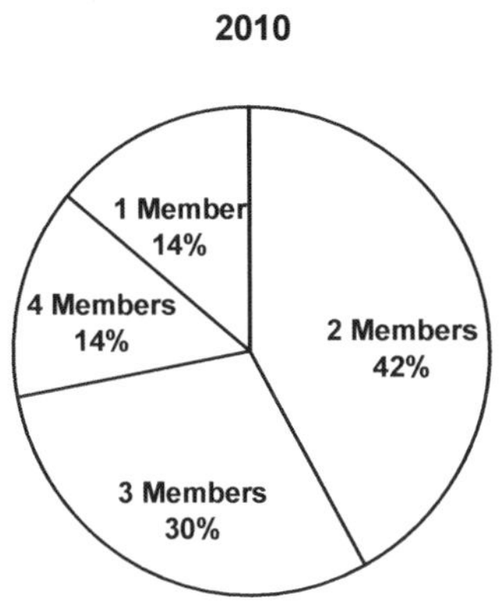

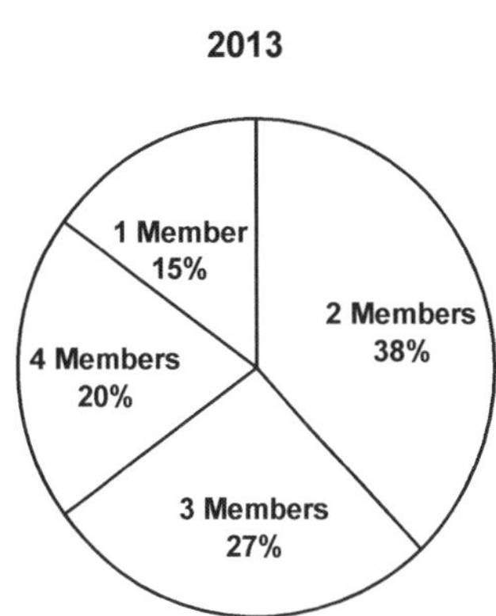

44. What is the total number of members, in millions, living in all families combined in 2010?

(A) 123.6

(B) 145.6

(C) 156.8

(D) 195.2

(E) 212.4

Solve yourself:

45. What is the approximate percent increase in the number of 4-Member families from 2010 to 2013?

(A) 30%

(B) 41%

(C) 56%

(D) 70%

(E) 74%

Solve yourself:

46. If $\left(\frac{1}{3}\right)^{\text{rd}}$ of the families in 2013 having only 1 member married (now counted in 2-member family), what would the actual percent of families having 2 members in the beginning of the next year? Assume that there is no other change in the distribution of the families from 2013.

(A) 33%

(B) 43%

(C) 45%

(D) 52%

(E) 60%

Solve yourself:

The following two questions are based on the following table.

The following table provides the data on oil production and petrol production of five countries in 2010 and 2011. All figures are in million tons.

Country	Oil production		Petrol production	
	2010	**2011**	**2010**	**2011**
USA	40000	45000	5000	6000
China	18000	20000	3200	4500
India	25000	30000	4500	6000
Iran	80000	84000	10000	15000
UAE	90000	96000	25000	30000

47. The total oil production in the world in 2011 was 450,000 million tons. What is the oil production by USA as a percent of the total oil production by the countries other than the five countries mentioned above?

(A) 10.0%
(B) 16.4%
(C) 25.7%
(D) 32.1%
(E) 41.2%

Solve yourself:

48. What is the production of petrol by the lowest two petrol producing countries as a percent of their oil production among the countries shown above in 2010?

(A) 14.2%
(B) 16.1%
(C) 17.9%
(D) 21.1%
(E) 23.3%

Solve yourself:

49. What is the production of oil by the highest two petrol producing countries among the countries shown as a percent of total oil production of five countries in 2011?

(A) 34.27%

(B) 46.16%

(C) 58.21%

(D) 65.45%

(E) 73.17%

Solve yourself:

The following two questions are based on the bar-graph and the line-graph below.

The chart below refers to three-year performance of the JP Chase Bank, in terms of Assets, in million dollars, and the number of Certificate Holders (CH), in millions.

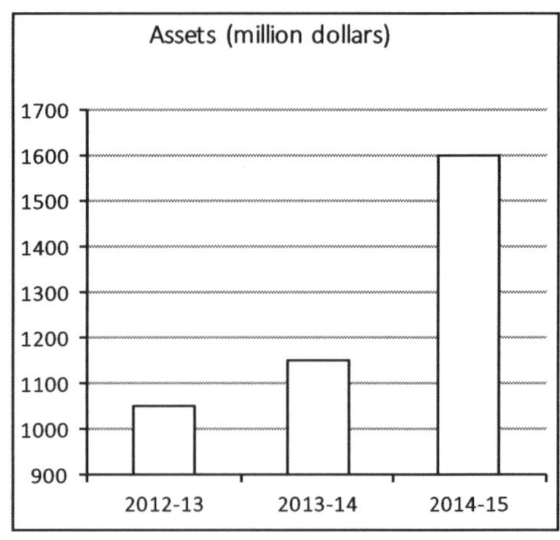

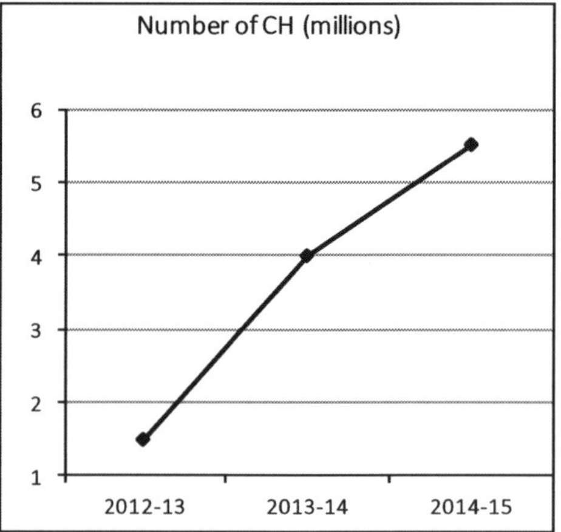

50. For a bank, a ratio of assets, in million dollars, to the number of certificate holders, in millions, equaling at least 320 is considered to be optimum. If in 2015-16, the number of certificate holders is expected to double from that in 2014-15, what should be the minimum assets of the bank so that the above ratio remains at optimum level?

(A) $35,200

(B) $352,000

(C) $3,520,000

(D) $3,520 million

(E) $35,200 million

Solve yourself:

51. The bank had to pay tax at a flat rate of 6% on its assets in 2014-15. If the tax rate was changed to 4% in 2015-16 and the tax paid by the bank should remain unchanged in 2015-16 compared to the tax paid in the previous year, what should be the assets of the bank, in million dollars, in 2015-16?

    (A) \$1800

    (B) \$2000

    (C) \$2400

    (D) \$2500

    (E) \$3600

    Solve yourself:

52. The mean of five integers is 10.2. If the least common multiple of the integers is 12, what could be the range of the set of integers?

    (A) 1

    (B) 3

    (C) 9

    (D) 10

    (E) 12

    Solve yourself:

53. In the set of five numbers $\{a^2, b^2, ab, a^2b, ab^2\}$, a and b represent positive integers with $a > b$. If the median of the above set of numbers is 45, what is the range of the above set?

(A) 30

(B) 45

(C) 60

(D) 66

(E) 75

Solve yourself:

The following two questions are based on the following bar-graph.

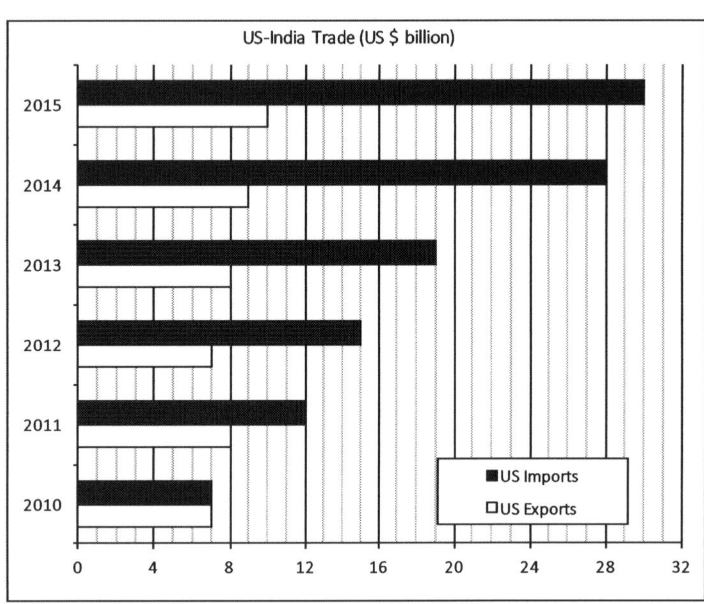

54. In which of the following years was the ratio of US exports to US imports minimum?

(A) 2011

(B) 2012

(C) 2013

(D) 2014

(E) 2015

Solve yourself:

55. What is the approximate value of the compounded average annual rate of increase in US imports from 2011 to 2015?

(A) 26%

(B) 36%

(C) 38%

(D) 50%

(E) 58%

Solve yourself:

3.2 Select One or Many Questions

56. Among the persons who attended a company meeting, some took only one glass of juice, some took only one glass of wine, while some took one glass of each. Of those who attended the meeting, 62 percent took one glass of wine and 53 percent did not take juice. If the total number of persons who attended the meeting be 100, what could be the number of people who took one glass of juice AND one glass of wine?

Indicate all such answers.

(A) 3
(B) 7
(C) 9
(D) 21
(E) 33
(F) 41
(G) 51

Solve yourself:

57. P is a set of consecutive positive integers from 1 to n. What is the difference between the median of the even numbers in the set and the median of the odd numbers in the set?

Indicate all possible answers.

(A) 0
(B) 1
(C) $\frac{n-1}{2}$
(D) $n-1$
(E) n

Solve yourself:

58. In the set of positive integers $\{2, 18, 4, 20, 19, 1, x, 21, 6\}$, if the median of the numbers is x and the mean of the numbers is between 11.5 and 12.5, exclusive, what is the value of x?

Indicate all possible values.

(A) 10
(B) 12
(C) 13
(D) 16
(E) 18
(F) 20

Solve yourself:

59. In a school, all students play at least one of the two games, rugby and baseball. 40% of all students play both rugby and baseball. If 20% of the students who play baseball do not play rugby, which of the following statements are correct?

Indicate all correct statements.

(A) 50% of the students play baseball
(B) 60% of the students play baseball
(C) 50% of the students play only rugby
(D) 90% of the students play rugby

Solve yourself:

60. In an examination, 36% of the candidates failed in Verbal Ability (VA) and 30% failed in Quantitative Aptitude (QA). What could be the percentage of those who passed in both VA and QA?

Indicate three possible values.

(A) 20%
(B) 30%
(C) 34%
(D) 50%
(E) 64%
(F) 70%

Solve yourself:

61. A group of people were asked to choose the TV show they liked between the two shows: GOT and COT. Of the total 30 people who put forward their choice, 18 chose GOT and 20 chose COT. If each person chooses at least one of the two shows, which of the following statements are correct?

Indicate all correct statements.

(A) 8 people liked both shows

(B) 22 people preferred one show over the other

(C) At least 12 people liked only COT

Solve yourself:

62. In a survey of college students, it was found that 50% preferred burgers, a few students preferred pizza and a few students preferred pasta. Of the total, 15% preferred ONLY pizza and 12% preferred ONLY pizza and pasta. Which of the following could be the percent of students who like ONLY pasta?

Indicate all possible values.

(A) 8

(B) 12

(C) 13

(D) 22

(E) 26

Solve yourself:

Following three questions are based on the following graph chart.

The graph shows the percentage of population owning TV sets in countries W, X, Y and Z.

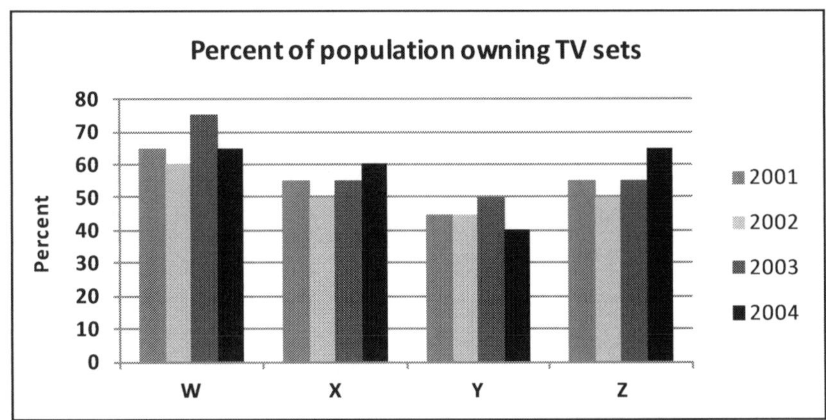

63. Assuming population in each of the years remained constant for each country, which country has shown the highest percent decline in the percent share of TV sets from 2001 to 2002?

Indicate all correct options.

(A) W

(B) X

(C) Y

(D) Z

Solve yourself:

64. Assuming that the population of all the countries is the same and remains constant for the given years, which of the following options are correct?

Indicate all correct options.

(A) Number of TV sets in X has increased by approximately 9% from 2001 to 2004.

(B) Number of TV sets in X in 2002 is the same as that in Y in 2003.

(C) Number of TV sets increased by approximately 4.5% per year for Z from 2001 to 2004.

(D) Total number of TV sets for all countries together increased by approximately 13.6% from 2001 to 2004.

Solve yourself:

65. Assuming that the population of each country increased by 10% per year over the given years, which of the following options are correct?

Indicate <u>all</u> correct options.

(A) Number of TV sets in Y has increased by 34.4% from 2001 to 2003.

(B) Among all countries, for the year 2001, the number of TV sets in country Y is the least.

(C) Number of TV sets decreased by 4.7% for W from 2003 to 2004.

Solve yourself:

66. In a set of 5 distinct positive integers, the median is 5 and the range is 5. If the mean of the numbers is greater than 5, which of the following numbers could belong in the set?

Indicate <u>all</u> possible numbers.

(A) 1

(B) 2

(C) 3

(D) 6

(E) 7

(F) 8

(G) 9

Solve yourself:

67. The numbers 4, 13, 8, a, 12, 3, 15, 22, 11, and 7 have a median value of 10. Which of the following CANNOT be the value of a?

Indicate all possible values.

(A) 7
(B) 8
(C) 9
(D) 10

Solve yourself:

68. In a set P, containing a few positive integers, the mean is m, range is r and the standard deviation is s. A positive constant k is added to each of the positive integers in set P to form a set Q. Now, the same constant k is multiplied to each of the positive integers of set P to form another set R. Which of the following statements is correct?

Indicate all possible statements.

(A) The mean of the set Q is $(m + k)$
(B) The range of the set Q is $(r + k)$
(C) The range of the set R is rk
(D) The standard deviation of the set Q is s
(E) The standard deviation of the set R is s

Solve yourself:

69. In a set of five positive integers, the smallest integer is 4. If mean of the five integers is 8, which of the following CANNOT be a possible value of the largest integer?

Indicate all possible values.

(A) 7
(B) 9
(C) 15
(D) 16
(E) 25

(F) 27

(G) 28

Solve yourself:

70. a, b, c, d, e, and f are six positive integers in ascending order, not necessarily distinct. The mean, median and mode of the six integers are p, q, and r, respectively. Which of the following statements may be correct?

Indicate <u>all</u> correct statements.

(A) $p = q = r$

(B) $q > 3p$

(C) $p = q + r$

Solve yourself:

3.3 Numeric Entry Questions

71. Each of 66 balls has an integer value, from 1 to 4, painted on it. The number of balls, n_i having a particular number i (1 through 4), painted on it, is given by the relation $n_i = 3 + (i+1)^2$. What is the Inter-Quartile Range (Difference between the Upper and Lower Quartiles of a set of data) of the 66 integers?

Solve yourself:

72. The average (arithmetic mean) of five different numbers is 12. If the median of the five numbers is equal to $\frac{1}{3}$ of the sum of the four numbers other than the median, what is the median of the five numbers?

Solve yourself:

73. The average (arithmetic mean) of four different numbers is 30. If none of the four numbers is greater than 33, what is the difference between the maximum possible value and the minimum possible value of the smallest number?

Solve yourself:

74. Bob has four different test scores. The median score is 80 and the range is 12. What is the maximum possible score he could have received on a test?

Solve yourself:

75. A student appeared for three tests. His mean score is 10 greater than his median score. If the range of scores of the student is 70 what is the difference between the median score and the lowest score?

Solve yourself:

76. The mean and the median of five distinct positive integers is 20. If the numbers are such that the product of the numbers is maximized, what is the product of the smallest and the largest integers?

Solve yourself:

77. The ages of the students in a university follow a normal distribution having a mean age of 24 years. If 47.5% of the students in the university have an age between 24 years and 28 years, what percent of the students, approximated to the nearest integer value, in the university have an age between 20 years and 22 years?

A normally distributed data is shown below:

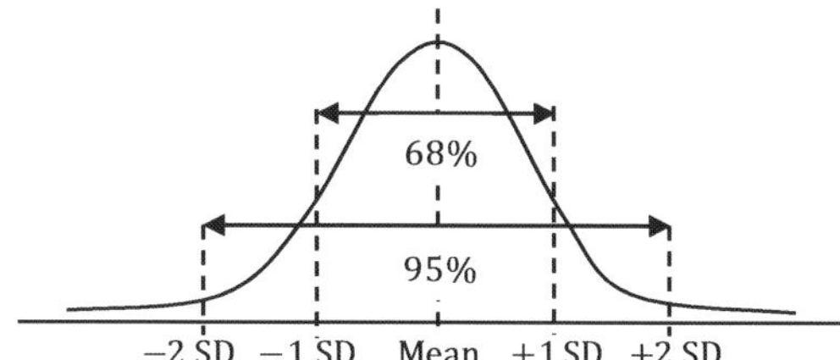

%

Solve yourself:

78. The average age of the students in a 'debate team' is 15 years. If the average age of the oldest three students is at least 17 years, and none of the students are younger than 12 years, what is the minimum number of students in the class? Assume that the ages of the students are integers.

Solve yourself:

79. The average of five distinct integers is 65. If the largest integer is 75, what is the maximum possible value of the smallest integer?

Solve yourself:

80. Four students contributed to a charity drive, and the average amount contributed by each student was \$20. If no student gave more than \$25 and all contributed different amounts, what is the maximum ratio of the amounts contributed by any two students?

$$\frac{\square}{\square}$$

Solve yourself:

81. The mean of 12 terms is x. If the first term is increased by 1, the second by 2, the third by 3, and so on, what is the increase in the value of the mean?

$\square$

Solve yourself:

82. For the set of numbers $\{x, y, (x + y), (x - 4y), xy, 2y\}$, the mean of the set equals $(y + 3)$. If $x + 2y = 22$, what is the median of the above set?

$\square$

Solve yourself:

83. The average of 7 numbers is 12. The average of the 4 smallest numbers in this set is 8, while the average of the 4 greatest numbers in this set is 20. How much is the sum of the 3 greatest numbers greater than the sum of the 3 smallest numbers?

$\square$

Solve yourself:

84. Five people have few marbles with them. The numbers of marbles with them are 23, 45, 51, 66 and 73. If they redistribute the marbles among themselves such that the number of marbles with each is a distinct integer and the median value of the number of marbles is maximized, what is the range of the number of marbles with them?

☐

Solve yourself:

85. The bar-graph below shows the expenditure, in thousand dollars, on marketing activities by two companies X and Y, for different years.

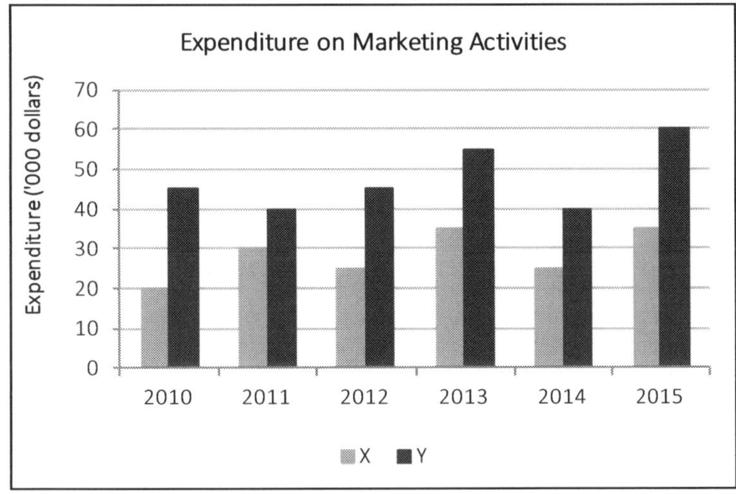

What is the highest ratio of the percent INCREASE in marketing expense of X and the percent INCREASE in marketing expense of Y in a particular year?

☐

Solve yourself:

3.4 Quantitative Comparison Questions

Options

Directions: Compare Quantity A and Quantity B, using additional information centered above the two quantities if such information is given, and select one of the following four answer choices:

(A) Quantity A is greater.

(B) Quantity B is greater.

(C) The two quantities are equal.

(D) The relationship cannot be determined from the information given.

A symbol that appears more than once in a question has the same meaning throughout the question.

86.

Each serving of:	Cost	Energy content
Tea	$5	3 kilocalories
Ice-cream	$20	240 kilocalories

A group of people consumed a number of servings of tea and a number of servings of ice-cream, thereby consuming a total of 966 kilocalories, which cost a total of $90. No person consumed both the items and each person took only one serving of any food item.

Quantity A	Quantity B
The number of people in the group	8

Solve yourself:

87. Each of the 45 boxes on shelf J weighs less than each of the 44 boxes on shelf K. The heaviest box on shelf J weighs 15 pounds.

Quantity A	Quantity B
The median weight of the 89 boxes on these shelves	15 pounds

Solve yourself:

88.

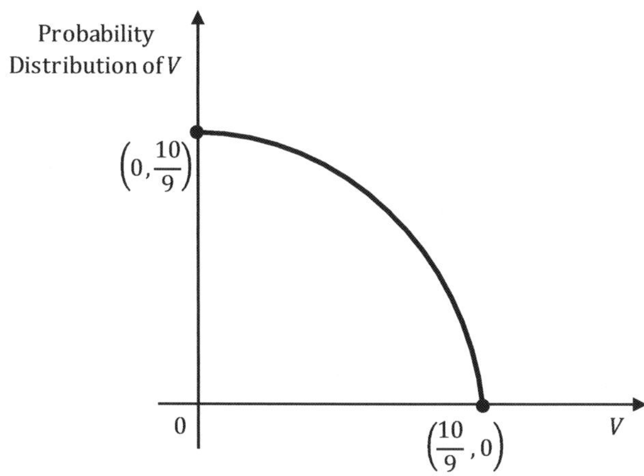

The above diagram shows the continuous probability distribution of the variable V in the range $0 < V < \frac{10}{9}$ in the coordinate plane with V on the horizontal axis. The probability distribution is a quadrant of a circle with radius $\frac{10}{9}$ and centre at the origin. (The value of π is assumed to be 3.24).

Quantity A	Quantity B
The median of the distribution of the variable V	$\frac{5}{9}$

Solve yourself:

89. The average (arithmetic mean) of 5 distinct integers is 17, and the least of these integers is -15.

Quantity A	Quantity B
The greatest among the above 5 integers	94

Solve yourself:

90. The average (arithmetic mean) of five positive integers is 7. The numbers have a single mode equal to 9.

Quantity A	Quantity B
The greatest possible value of the smallest term	4

Solve yourself:

91. The average (arithmetic mean) of 8 consecutive odd integers is 36.

Quantity A	Quantity B
Twice the value of the greatest term	Thrice the value of the smallest term

Solve yourself:

92. The expenditures and revenues of a company for five months is shown in the table below. The gross profit for any month equals revenue minus expenditure for that month.

Month	Expenditure ('000 dollars)	Revenue ('000 dollars)
January	130	160
February	120	140
March	110	120
April	140	160
May	150	180

Quantity A	Quantity B
The median value of the Gross Profit	\$20,000

Solve yourself:

93. Cards numbered 1 to 20 are randomly grouped to form four groups of five cards each.

Quantity A	**Quantity B**
The maximum possible sum of the median numbers of the four groups	40

Solve yourself:

94. The average (arithmetic mean) of five integers: 2, p, q, r and 10, is three times the median. It is known that $10 > r > q > p > 2$.

Quantity A	**Quantity B**
The maximum value of $\left(\frac{r}{q}\right)$	$12\frac{1}{3}$

Solve yourself:

95. The average of five distinct integers is 12, and the smallest of the six integers is 4.

Quantity A	Quantity B
The number of possible values that exist for the largest of the five integers	Ten

Solve yourself:

96. $2p$, $2p + 1$, $3p$, $4p - 1$ and $4p + 5$ are five numbers in a set. The average of the five numbers is 10.

Quantity A	Quantity B
The median of the five integers	9

Solve yourself:

97.

Quantity A	Quantity B
The standard deviation of the set {1, 5, 7, 19}	The standard deviation of the set {0, 5, 7, 20}

Solve yourself:

98. In a class, the range of the heights of the boys is 10 inches and the range of the heights of the girls is 8 inches.

Quantity A	Quantity B
The range of the heights of the boys and girls taken together	10 inches

Solve yourself:

99. For a group of test takers, the scores on an aptitude test were normally distributed. It had a mean of 74, and a standard deviation of 4.

Quantity A	Quantity B
The fraction of test takers in the group who scored greater than 81	$\frac{1}{5}$

Solve yourself:

100. The average (arithmetic mean) of four different positive integers is 12. The sum of the four integers and their median is 58.

Quantity A	Quantity B
The average (arithmetic mean) of the smallest and the largest numbers	14

Solve yourself:

Chapter 4

Answer-key

Multiple Choice Questions

(1) C	(15) B	(29) B	(43) A
(2) D	(16) D	(30) C	(44) D
(3) D	(17) C	(31) A	(45) D
(4) A	(18) B	(32) E	(46) B
(5) A	(19) A	(33) B	(47) C
(6) B	(20) D	(34) B	(48) C
(7) D	(21) B	(35) C	(49) D
(8) B	(22) A	(36) C	(50) D
(9) E	(23) A	(37) A	(51) C
(10) D	(24) D	(38) C	(52) C
(11) A	(25) D	(39) D	(53) D
(12) B	(26) C	(40) B	(54) D
(13) B	(27) D	(41) D	(55) A
(14) D	(28) B	(42) E	

Select One or Many

(56) C, D, E, & F	(60) C, D, & E	(64) A & B	(68) A, C, & D
(57) A & B	(61) A, B, & C	(65) A & C	(69) A, E, F, & G
(58) C, D, & E	(62) A, B, C, & D	(66) C, D, E, & F	(70) A & C
(59) A, C, & D	(63) B & D	(67) A, B, & D	

Numeric Entry Questions

(71) 2

(72) 15

(73) 4

(74) 90

(75) 20

(76) 396

(77) 13.5

(78) 5

(79) 61

(80) $\frac{25}{8}$

(81) 6.5

(82) 11

(83) 48

(84) 85

(85) 1.8

Quantitative Comparison Questions

(86) B

(87) C

(88) B

(89) A

(90) C

(91) B

(92) C

(93) A

(94) B

(95) A

(96) C

(97) B

(98) D

(99) B

(100) C

Chapter 5

Solutions

5.1 Multiple Choice Questions

1. The above information can be represented in a Venn-diagram as shown below:

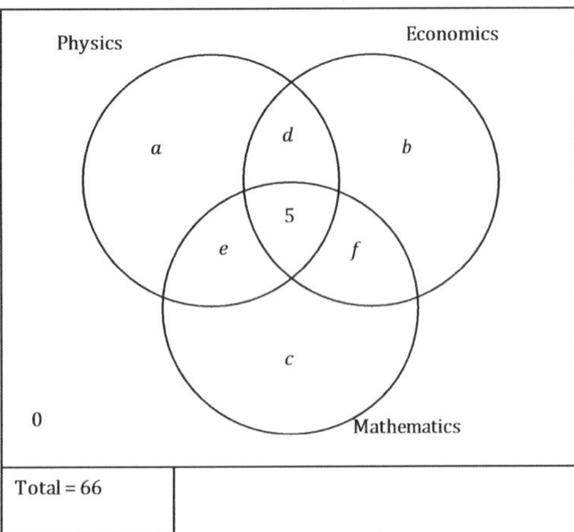

Thus, we have:

- 28 students did not choose either Physics or Economics

  $=> c = 28 \ldots \text{(i)}$

- 15 students did not choose either Mathematics or Economics

  $=> a = 15 \ldots \text{(ii)}$

- 45 students did not choose Economics

  $=> a + c + e = 45$

  $=> e = 45 - (a + c) = 45 - (28 + 15)$

  $=> e = 2 \ldots \text{(iii)}$

- 30 students did not choose Mathematics

  $=> a + d + b = 30$

  $=> d + b = 30 - a = 30 - 15 => d + b = 15 \ldots \text{(iv)}$

- Number of students who did not choose either Mathematics or Economics, exceeded the number of students who did not choose Mathematics or Physics by 2

  $=> a = b + 2$

  $=> b = a - 2 = 15 - 2 => b = 13 \ldots \text{(v)}$

  Thus, from (iv), we have:

  $d = 15 - b = 15 - 13$

  $=> d = 2 \ldots \text{(vi)}$

- Total number of students is 66

  => $a + b + c + d + e + f + 5 = 66$

  => $f = 66 - (a + b + c + d + e + 5) = 66 - (15 + 13 + 28 + 2 + 2 + 5)$

  => $f = 1$

Thus, the number of students who chose both Economics and Mathematics

$= f + 5 = 1 + 5 = 6$

The complete Venn-diagram is shown below for reference:

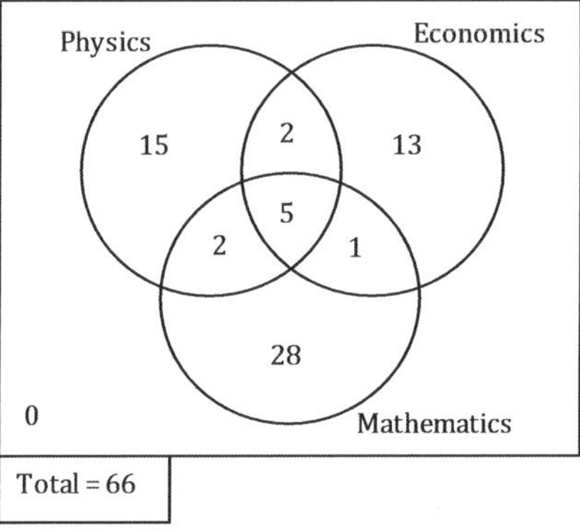

The correct answer is option C.

2. The data can be represented in a Venn-diagram as shown below:

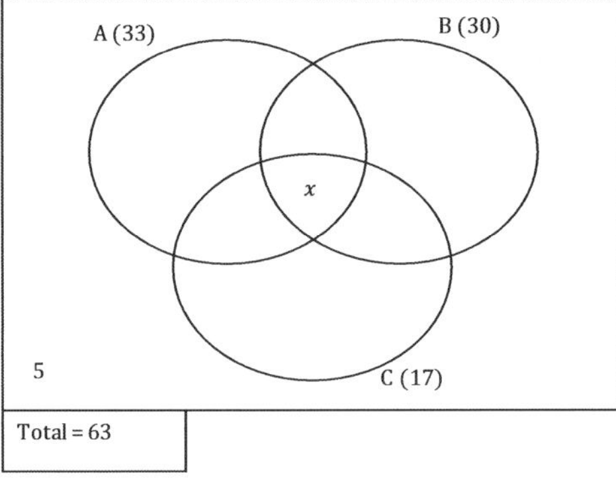

The meaning of "For any two of the magazines, 9 people subscribed to both the magazines." is that

A & B = B & C = A & C = 9

Also, we know that:

A or B or C = 63 − 5 = 58; given that 5 people did not subscribe any magazine.

Thus, we have:

A or B or C = A + B + C− (A & B + B & C + A & C) + A & B & C

$=> 58 = 33 + 30 + 17 - (9 + 9 + 9) + x$

$=> 58 = 80 - 27 + x$

$=> x = 5$

The correct answer is option D.

Alternate Approach:

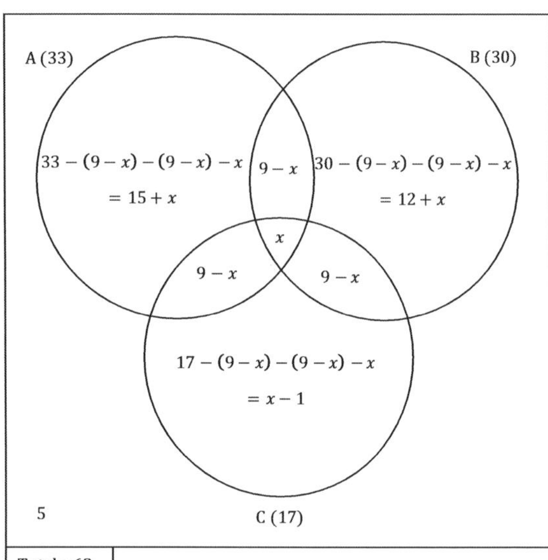

Based on the Venn-diagram shown above, we have:

$(15 + x) + (12 + x) + (x - 1) + (9 - x) + (9 - x) + (9 - x) + x + 5 = 63$

$=> 58 + x = 63$

$=> x = 5$

3. Let us present the data in Venn diagram.

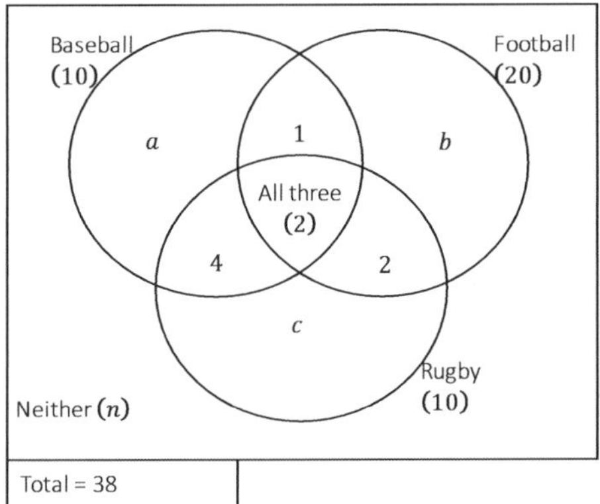

We have:

$a = 10 - (4 + 2 + 1) = 3$

$b = 20 - (2 + 2 + 1) = 15$

$c = 10 - (4 + 2 + 2) = 2$

$n = 38 - (a + b + c + 4 + 2 + 2 + 1) = 38 - (3 + 15 + 2 + 9) = 9$

The correct answer is option D.

4. The students who failed in at least 2 subjects = The students who failed in exactly 2 subjects + The students who failed in all 3 subjects

=> 13 = (The students who failed in exactly 2 subjects) + 5

=> The students who failed in exactly 2 subjects = 8

=> The number of students who passed in only 1 subject = 8 . . . (i)

The students who failed in at least 1 subject = The students who failed in exactly 1 subject + The students who failed in exactly 2 subjects + The students who failed in all 3 subjects

=> 24 = (The students who failed in exactly 1 subject) + 8 + 5

=> The students who failed in exactly 1 subject = 11

=> The number of students who passed in only 2 subjects = 11 . . . (ii)

Thus, from (i) and (ii):

The required difference = 11 - 8 = 3

The correct answer is option A.

5. Let us present the data in Venn diagram.

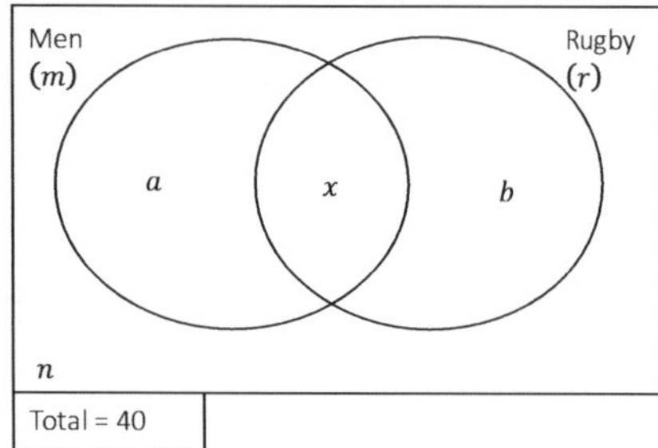

Since the total number of employees is 40, we have:

Number of women = 25% of 40 = 10

$=> 40 - m = 10$

$=> m = 30$

We also have:

$x = 33.33\%$ of $m = 50\%$ of r

$=> x = \frac{m}{3} = \frac{r}{2}$

$=> x = \frac{30}{3} = 10$

$=> \frac{r}{2} = 10 => r = 20$

Thus, we have:

$n = 40 - (m + r - x) = 40 - (30 + 20 - 10) = 0$

Thus, the number of women who do not play rugby = $n = 0$

The correct answer is option A.

6. Let us present the data in Venn diagram.

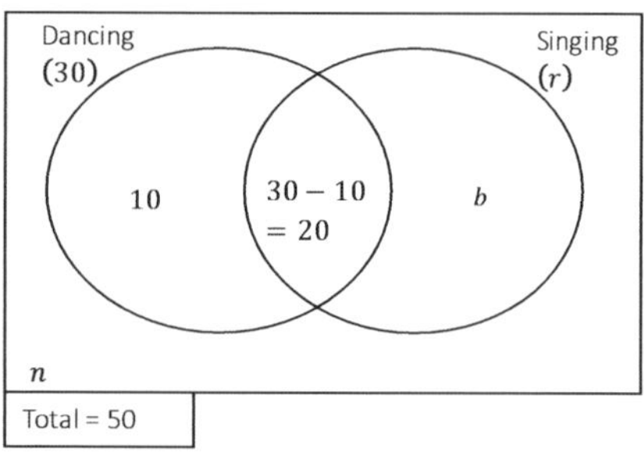

Since 20 students do not like singling, we have:

$n + 10 = 20$

$=> n = 10$

Since there are 50 students, we have:

$30 + r - 20 = 50 - n$

$=> 10 + r = 40$

$=> r = 30$

$=> b = r - 20 = 10$

Thus, the number of students who do not like dancing but like singing = $b = 10$

The correct answer is option B.

7. Let us analyze the situations of John and Bob:

John:

John's score = 75

Mean score of all students = 70

Difference between John's score and the mean score = 75 - 70 = 5

Standard deviation of all scores = 2

Thus, number of 'Standard deviations' that John's score is more than the mean score = $\frac{5}{2} = 2.5$

Bob:

Bob's score = 72

Mean score of all students = 65

Difference between Bob's score and the mean score = 72 - 65 = 7

Standard deviation of all scores = 3

Thus, number of 'Standard deviations' that Bob's score is more than the mean score = $\frac{7}{3} = 2.33$

Thus, John's score (2.5 times standard deviation more) is farther away from the mean than is Bob's score (2.33 times standard deviation more).

Thus, John ranks higher in his class than Bob does in his class. - Statement I is correct

Considering statement II:

Since John's score is higher than the mean score, there may or may not be a student who scored higher than what John has scored. - Statement II is incorrect

Considering statement III:

Since Bob's score is higher than the mean score, there must be at least one student who scored less than the mean score, and hence, scored less than Bob's score. - Statement III is correct

The correct answer is option D.

8. Since the average of the five positive integers is 16, we have:

$$\frac{k+m+r+s+t}{5} = 16$$
$$=> k+m+r+s+t = 80$$

Since $t = 40$, we have:

$k+m+r+s = 80 - 40 = 40 \ldots$ (i)

Also, we have:
$k < m < r < s < t$

$=> k < m < r < s < 40$

The median is the middle term when the numbers are arranged in order.

Thus, the median is r.

Since we need to maximize r, and time keep all the numbers positive integers, we have:

$k = 1, \ m = 2$

Thus, from (i), we have:
$r + s = 40 - (1 + 2) = 37$

Since $r < s$, we have:
$s = (r + 1)$

$r = 18, \ s = 19$

Thus, the maximum value of the median is 18.

The correct answer is option B.

9. Let us bring out the graph.

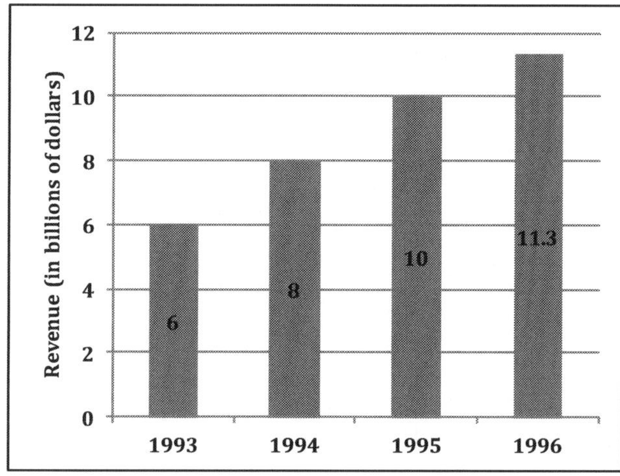

Revenue of the particular store in 1994

= 2% of Combined revenue in 1994

$= \frac{2}{100} \times 8$

= \$0.16 billion

Revenue of the store in 1995

= 2.3% of Combined revenue in 1995

$= \frac{2.3}{100} \times 10$

= \$0.23 billion

Thus, percent increase in revenue of the store

$= \frac{0.23 - 0.16}{0.16} \times 100\%$

$= \frac{0.07}{0.16} \times 100\%$

= 43.75%

The correct answer is option E.

10. Say the score in the sixth test = n

Thus, the scores in the six tests are = 43, 47, 39, 27, 34, and n, respectively.

Thus, the total score = 43 + 47 + 39 + 27 + 34 + n = 190 + n

Thus, the mean score = $\frac{190 + n}{6}$

We know that the mean score and the median score are the same.

Working with the statements:

I. $n = 29$:

Mean = $\frac{190 + 29}{6} = \frac{219}{6} = 36.5$

The scores, when arranged in order, are: 27, 29, 34, 39, 43, and 47

The median is the average of the two middle terms.

Thus, we have:

$$\text{Median} = \frac{\left\{\left(\frac{6}{2}\right)^{\text{th}} \text{term} + \left(\frac{6}{2} + 1\right)^{\text{th}} \text{term}\right\}}{2} = \frac{\{3^{\text{rd}} \text{ term} + 4^{\text{th}} \text{ term}\}}{2}$$

$$= \frac{34 + 39}{2} = \frac{73}{2} = 36.5$$

Thus, Mean = Median - Satisfies

II. $n = 36$:

Mean = $\frac{190 + 36}{6} = \frac{226}{6} = 37.67$

The scores, when arranged in order, are: 27, 34, 36, 39, 43, and 47

The median is the average of the two middle terms.

Thus, we have:

$$\text{Median} = \frac{\left\{\left(\frac{6}{2}\right)^{\text{th}} \text{term} + \left(\frac{6}{2} + 1\right)^{\text{th}} \text{term}\right\}}{2} = \frac{\{3^{\text{rd}} \text{ term} + 4^{\text{th}} \text{ term}\}}{2}$$

$$= \frac{36 + 39}{2} = \frac{73}{2} = 36.5$$

Thus, Mean $\neq$ Median - Does not satisfy

III. $n = 56$:

Mean = $\frac{190 + 56}{6} = \frac{246}{6} = 41$

The scores, when arranged in order, are: 27, 34, 39, 43, 47, and 56

The median is the average of the two middle terms.

Thus, we have:

$$\text{Median} = \frac{\left\{\left(\frac{6}{2}\right)^{\text{th}}\text{term} + \left(\frac{6}{2}+1\right)^{\text{th}}\text{term}\right\}}{2} = \frac{\left\{3^{\text{rd}}\text{ term} + 4^{\text{th}}\text{ term}\right\}}{2}$$

$$= \frac{39+43}{2} = \frac{82}{2} = 41$$

Thus, Mean = Median - Satisfies

The correct answer is option D.

11.

Car Brand	Sales
A	500
B	350
C	160
D	290
E	150
Total	**1450**

Since these five car brands represent 30% of the city's sales, the car brands not shown in the table above represent (100 - 30) = 70% of the city's sales.

Let the city's sales of all the car brands be s.

Thus, we have:

1450 = 30% of s

$$=> 1450 = \frac{3}{10}s$$

$$=> s = \frac{14500}{3} \ldots \text{(i)}$$

Thus, sales of the other car brands = 70% of $s = \frac{7}{10}s$.

We need to determine the value of sales of car brand D as a percent of the sales of the other car brands, i.e.

$$\left(\frac{\text{Sale of car brand D}}{\text{Sale of other car brands}}\right)\times 100$$

$$= \frac{290}{\left(\frac{7}{10}s\right)} \times 100\%$$

$$= \frac{2900}{7s} \times 100\%$$

Using (i), we have:

Required percent value

$$= \frac{2900}{\left(7 \times \frac{14500}{3}\right)} \times 100\%$$

$$= \frac{29 \times 3}{145 \times 7} \times 100\%$$

$$= \frac{3}{5 \times 7} \times 100\%$$

$$= \frac{60}{7}\%$$

$$=\approx 8.57\%$$

Note: The calculation of s and the calculation of the sale of the other car brands have been avoided.

The correct answer is option A.

12. Brand Speedex:

Price per gallon = \$2.50

Thus, quantity of gasoline obtained for \$50

$$= \frac{50}{2.50}$$

= 20 gallons

Distance covered per gallon = 50 miles

Thus, distance covered using 20 gallons = 20 × 50 = 1000 miles.

Brand Zoomex:

Price per gallon = \$2.20

Thus, quantity of gasoline obtained for \$50

$$= \frac{50}{2.20}$$

$$= \frac{250}{11} \text{ gallons}$$

Distance covered per gallon = 33 miles

Thus, distance covered using $\frac{250}{11}$ gallons = $\frac{250}{11} \times 33 = 750$ miles.

Thus, the required difference = 1000 - 750 = 250 miles.

The correct answer is option B.

13.

Brand	**Sales, 2015**	**Percent change from 2014**
X	96	−20%
Y	246	−18%
Z	288	+20%
P	480	+200%
Q	100	+25%

Let the percent change from 2014 to 2015 be $p\%$

Thus, we have:

$$\text{Sales in 2015} = (\text{Sales in 2014}) \times \left(1 \pm \frac{p}{100}\right)$$

$$\Rightarrow \text{Sales in 2014} = \frac{\text{Sales in 2015}}{\left(1 \pm \frac{p}{100}\right)}$$

In the relation above, (+) is used if the percent change is positive and (−) is used if the percent change is negative.

Thus, based on the above relation, we have:

Brand	Sales in 2015	Percent change from 2014	Sales in 2014
X	96	−20%	$\frac{96}{\left(1-\frac{20}{100}\right)}=\frac{96}{0.8}=120$
Y	246	−18%	$\frac{246}{\left(1-\frac{18}{100}\right)}=\frac{246}{0.82}=300$ **(Greatest)**
Z	288	+20%	$\frac{288}{\left(1+\frac{20}{100}\right)}=\frac{288}{1.2}=240$
P	480	+200%	$\frac{480}{\left(1+\frac{200}{100}\right)}=\frac{480}{3}=160$
Q	100	+25%	$\frac{100}{\left(1+\frac{25}{100}\right)}=\frac{100}{1.25}=80$

The correct answer is option B.

14. We are given that the number of sales interactions made each month was proportional to the number of cars sold in that month

Thus, we have:

Number of calls interactions in a month = $k\times$(Number of cars sold in that month)

In the relation above, k is a constant of proportionality.

Thus, we have:

Month	Number of cars sold	number of sales interactions
January	13	$13k$
February	18	$18k$
March	27	$27k$
April	16	$16k$

Since the total number of calls made is 222, we have:

$13k + 18k + 27k + 16k = 222$

$=> k = \frac{222}{74} = 3$

Thus, the number of sales interactions made in April

$= 16k = 16 \times 3 = 48$

The correct answer is option D.

15. The median of a set of data is the value of the middle term (if there are an odd number of data values) or the average of the two middle terms (if there are an even number of data values) after arranging the data in ascending or descending order.

Here, the number of defects in a batch are arranged in ascending order.

Number of data values is 81, which is an odd number.

Thus, the median would be the middle term, i.e. $\left(\frac{81+1}{2}\right)^{th}$ term, i.e. the 41st term (batch).

Counting the number of terms from the beginning, the 41st term (batch) falls under '10 - 14' class as shown below:

Number of defects	**Number of batches**	**Cumulative number of batches**
Less than 5	18	18
5 - 9	17	18 + 17 = 35
10 - 14	23	**35 + 23 = 58 => 41st batch falls in this class**
15 - 19	8	
20 - 24	9	
25 - 29	6	
30 and above	2	

The correct answer is option B.

16. If the 15 different integers are arranged in order, the median is the $\left(\frac{15+1}{2}\right)^{th} = 8^{th}$ integer.

Thus, the 8th integer is 30.

Since we need to find the integer with the greatest possible value (given a constant range of 30), we must have the maximum possible value of the least integer as well.

Since the integers are distinct, we can have the first 8 integers as:

$(30-7) = 23$, $(30-6) = 24$, $(30-5) = 25$, $(30-4) = 26$, $(30-3) = 27$, $(30-2) = 28$, $(30-1) = 29$ and 30

Thus, the maximum value of the smallest integer = 23.

Since the range is 30, the value of the greatest integer = 23 + 30 = 53.

The correct answer is option D.

17. We have Mean = $\left(\frac{\text{Sum of the terms}}{\text{Total number of terms}}\right)$

=> $\frac{3+2+6+8+5+x}{6} = \frac{x^2}{2}$

=> $\frac{24+x}{6} = \frac{x^2}{2}$

=> $24 + x = 3x^2$

=> $3x^2 - x - 24 = 0$

=> $(3x + 8)(x - 3) = 0$

=> $x = -\frac{8}{3}$ or 3

Since x is an integer, we have: $x = 3$

Thus, the set of integers = {3, 4, 4, 5, 5, 6}.

Thus, the range = 6 − 3 = 3.

The correct answer is option C.

18. We know that there are x members, where x is an odd number.

The median value of x terms, where x is odd, is given by:

Median = $\left(\frac{x+1}{2}\right)^{\text{th}}$ term

Thus, we have:

$\frac{x+1}{2} = 21$

=> $x = 43$

Thus, there are 43 members in the club.

Thus, the average age of the members in the club

$= \dfrac{\text{Total age}}{\text{Number of members}}$

$= \left(\dfrac{1720}{43}\right)$

$= 40$

The correct answer is option B.

19. Say there were x millions numbers of microbes on Day 2.

Let's ignore minions for the sake of calculations.

Increase in the count of microbes from Day 1 to Day 2 = $(x - 10)$.

Thus, fractional increase

$= \dfrac{\text{Increase}}{\text{Original value}}$

$= \left(\dfrac{x - 10}{10}\right)$

Increase in the numbers of microbes from Day 2 to Day 3 = $(14.4 - x)$.

Thus, fractional increase

$= \dfrac{\text{Increase}}{\text{Original value}}$

$= \left(\dfrac{14.4 - x}{x}\right)$

Since the fractional increases are the same, we have:

$\dfrac{x - 10}{10} = \dfrac{14.4 - x}{x}$

$=> \dfrac{x}{10} - 1 = \dfrac{14.4}{x} - 1$

$=> \dfrac{x}{10} = \dfrac{14.4}{x}$

$=> x^2 = 14.4 \times 10$

$=> x^2 = 144$

$=> x = 12$ millions

The correct answer is option A.

Alternate Approach I:

Since the numbers of microbes increased by the same proportion during each of the two day periods, we can say that the ratio of the numbers of microbes in consecutive intervals would be equal.

Thus we have:

$$\frac{10.0}{x} = \frac{x}{14.4}$$

$=> x^2 = 14.4 \times 10.0$

$=> x^2 = 144$

$=> x = 12.0$ millions

Alternate Approach II:

Since the fractional increase in each two-day period is the same, we can conclude that the percent change in each two-day period is also the same.

Let the percent change be p.

Thus, using the concept of compound interest, we have:

$$14.4 = 10 \times \left(1 + \frac{p}{100}\right)^2$$

$$=> \left(1 + \frac{p}{100}\right)^2 = 1.44 = 1.2^2$$

$$=> 1 + \frac{p}{100} = 1.2$$

$$=> p = 20\%$$

$$=> x = 10 \times \left(1 + \frac{20}{100}\right)^1 = 12 \text{ millions}$$

20. We can calculate the average sale value, in dollars, per bike as shown below:

Bikes sold by a store on July 4			
Type of bikes	Number of bikes sold	Price per bike (dollars)	Total Price of bikes (dollars)
52"	5	190	$5 \times 190 = 900$
54"	7	210	$7 \times 210 = 1470$
56"	10	340	$10 \times 340 = 3400$
58"	12	360	$12 \times 360 = 4320$
Total	34 bikes		10,090

Thus, the approximate average sale value, in dollars, per bike

$$= \frac{10090}{34} =\approx \frac{10000}{33.33} =\approx \frac{100 \times 100}{33.33} =\approx 100 \times \frac{100}{33.33} =\approx 100 \times 3 =\approx \$300.$$

The closest answer to \$300 is \$297. The answers \$233 is too less and \$348 is too greater to \$300, thus, they cannot be the contenders.

The correct answer is option D.

21. Loan Sanctions as a percent of Total Revenue for Bank X

$= \frac{650}{1600} \times 100\%$

$= \frac{650}{16}\%$

$= 40.625\%$

Loan Sanctions as a percent of Total Revenue for Bank Y

$= \frac{1500}{3500} \times 100\%$

$= \frac{15}{35} \times 100\%$

$= \frac{300}{7}\%$

$= 42.85\%$

Thus, the required positive difference
$= 42.85 - 40.625$

$= 2.225 =\approx 2.2$

The correct answer is option B.

22. Percent increase in Net Profit from 2010 to 2011

$= \frac{(\text{Net Profit in 2011}) - (\text{Net Profit in 2010})}{(\text{Net Profit in 2011})} \times 100$

$= \frac{150 - 125}{125} \times 100\%$

$= \frac{25}{125} \times 100$

$= 20\%$

Thus, the percent increase in Net Profit from 2011 to 2012 = 20%

Thus, Net Profit in 2012

$= (100 + 20)\%$ of Net Profit in 2011

$= 120\%$ of (\$150 million)

$= \$\left(\frac{120}{100} \times 150\right)$ million

$= \$180$ million

Total Income in 2012 is double the Total Income in 2011

=> Total Income in 2012 $= 2 \times (\$450$ million)

$= \$900$ million

Thus, the required ratio

$$= \frac{180}{900}$$

$$= \frac{1}{5}$$

The correct answer is option A.

23. We know that the average number of correct answers was 50 and the median number of correct answers was 40.

Since there were 9 candidates, the median value would be that for the $\left(\frac{9+1}{2}\right)^{\text{th}} = 5^{\text{th}}$ student (after arranging in ascending or descending order).

Let the average of the number of correct answers of the first 4 students be f, and the average of the number of correct answers of the last 4 students be l.

Since the average number of correct answers is 50, we have:

$$\frac{4f + 40 + 4l}{9} = 50$$

$=> 4f + 4l = 410$

$=> f + l = 102.5 \ldots$ (i)

Since the number of correct answers of the first four students must be less than or equal to 40, we have:

$f \leq 40$

Thus, from (i):

$l \geq 102.5 - 40 = 62.5$

Thus, the average number of correct answers of the last 4 students is at least 62.5

Thus, at least one student must have got more than 60 correct answers.

Thus, statement I is definitely correct.

However, the other statements may or may not be correct. Say, 8 students got 40 each and the 9th got 90, maintaining the average equal to 50. Thus, in this scenario, none falls in the condition stated in II and in III.

The correct answer is option A.

24. Let's bring out the graph.

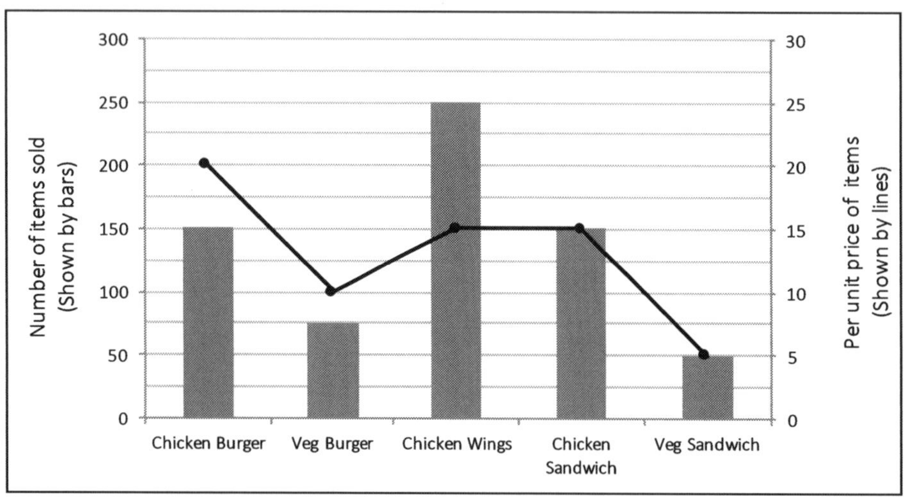

In order to determine the median price, we first need to arrange the food items according to ascending or descending order of their prices. Thus, we have the following table:

Food item	**Price per unit ($)**	**Number of units sold**	**Cumulative number of units**	
Veg burger	10	75	75	
Veg sandwich	5	50	125	
Chicken wings	**15**	**250**	**375**	**<— 338th item**
Chicken sandwich	15	150	525	
Chicken burger	20	150	675	
TOTAL	-	**675**		

Since the number of items sold is 675, the median value

$= \text{Price of the} \left(\frac{675+1}{2}\right)^{\text{th}} \text{item}$

$= \text{Price of the } 338^{\text{th}} \text{ item} = \$15$

The correct answer is option D.

The following three questions are based on the following bar chart.

The following graph shows the percent distribution of the number of employees of a company from 2010 to 2013 in four departments: R&D, HR, Sales and Finance.

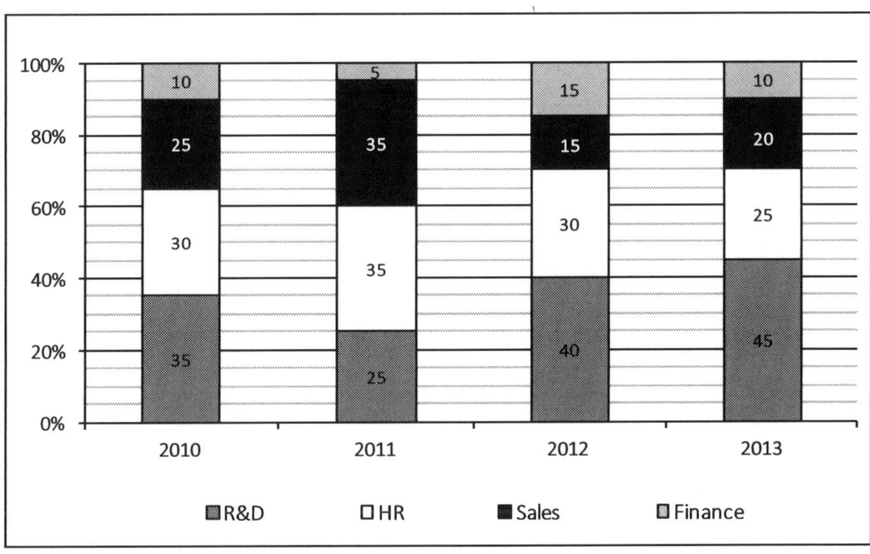

25. Let the number of employees in each year be 100.

Number of employees in R&D in 2010 = 35% of 100 = 35

Number of employees in R&D in 2013 = 45% of 100 = 45

Thus, percent increase = $\left(\frac{45 - 35}{35}\right) \times 100 = 28.6\%$

This increase happened over a period of 3 years: 2010-2011, 2011-2012 and 2012-2013.

Thus, the simple annual percent increase = $\frac{28.6}{3} = 9.53\%$

The correct answer is option D.

26. We know that the total number of employees in 2011 was 2500.

Since every year the percent increase in the number of employees is 20%, the number of employees in 2012 = 120% of 2500 = 3000

Similarly, number of employees in 2013 = 120% of 3000 = 3600

Thus, the number of employees in the Finance department in 2013

= 10% of 3600 = 360

The correct answer is option C.

Alternate Approach:

Alternatively, you can calculate it as following:

$S_{2013} = S_{2011}(1 + r\%)^n$

$S_{2013} = 2500(1 + 20\%)^2$

$S_{2013} = 2500\left(1 + \frac{1}{5}\right)^2 = 2500(1.2)^2 = 2500 \times 1.44 = 3600$

Thus, the number of employees in the Finance department in 2013

= 10% of 3600 = 360.

27. The answer must be one of the options given. So, it is sufficient to check each option and determine the maximum percent increase among those.

Let the total number of employees in each year be 100. Thus, the percent values in the bar-graph represent the actual number of employees in each year.

Working with the options:

- Option A: Sales, 2011 over Sales, 2010: Percent increase $= \frac{35 - 25}{25} \times 100 = 40\%$
- Option B: HR, 2011 over HR, 2010: Percent increase $= \frac{35 - 30}{30} \times 100 = 16.7\%$
- Option C: R&D, 2012 over R&D, 2011: Percent increase $= \frac{40 - 25}{25} \times 100 = 60\%$
- Option D: Finance, 2012 over Finance, 2011: Percent increase $= \frac{15 - 5}{5} \times 100 = 200\%$
- Option E: Sales, 2013 over Sales, 2012: Percent increase $= \frac{20 - 15}{15} \times 100 = 33.3\%$

Alternately, one could just observe the bar-graph and observe that the shaded region for Finance has seen the greatest proportion increase from 2011 to 2012 (the increased value is thrice of the initial value). Thus, the maximum percent increase must be for Finance from 2011 to 2012.

The correct answer is option D.

The following two questions are based on the following bar chart.

The graphs below show some information regarding the US-China trade from 2005-2010.

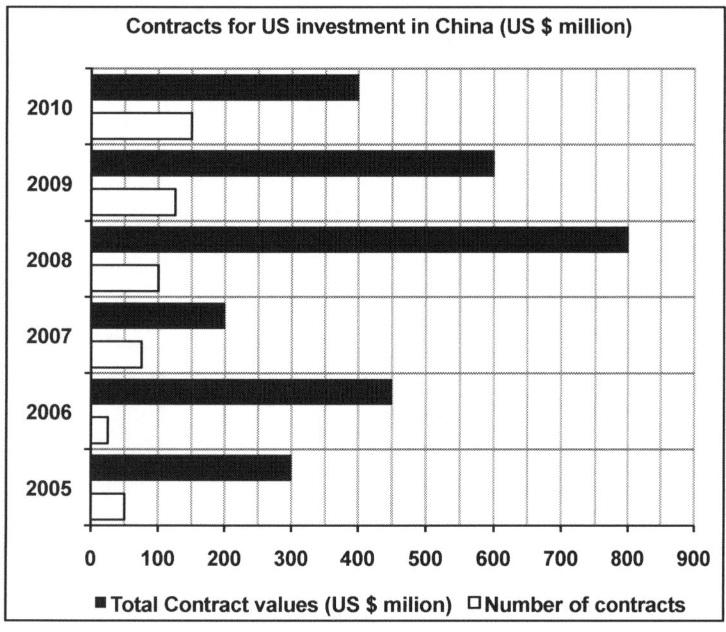

28. From the bar-graph, we have:

- In 2005:

  Number of contracts = 50

  Total value of all contracts = \$300 million

  Thus, average value of a contract = $\$\left(\frac{300}{50}\right)$ million = \$6 million

- In 2010:

  Number of contracts = 150

  Total value of all contracts = \$400 million

  Thus, average value of a contract = $\$\left(\frac{400}{150}\right)$ million = \$2.67 million

Thus, percent decrease = $\left(\frac{6-2.67}{6}\right) \times 100\% = 55.5\%$

The correct answer is option B.

29. Working with the statements:

- Option A:

  From the graph, we observe that the number of contracts decreased from 2005 to 2006 and then for each of the remaining years, they increased.

In no two consecutive years, did the number of contracts remain the same. - Correct

- Option B:

  From the graph, we observe for 2006-2007, 2008-2009, and 2009-2010, the number of contracts increased, while the value of the contracts decreased. - Incorrect

  Thus, the correct answer should be option B. However, let us verify the other options as well:

- Option C:

  From the graph, we observe that:

  - From 2005-2006: The number of contracts decreased
  - From 2006-2007: The number of contracts increased by $75 - 25 = 50$
  - For each of the other years: The number of contracts increased by 25

  Thus, the greatest increase in the number of contracts was in 2007 over 2006. - Correct

- Option D:

  Total number of contracts $= 50 + 25 + 75 + 100 + 125 + 150 = 525$. - Correct

The correct answer is option B.

The following four questions are based on the following bar chart.

The graph shows the exports of iron-ore from country X from January 2001 to December 2001.

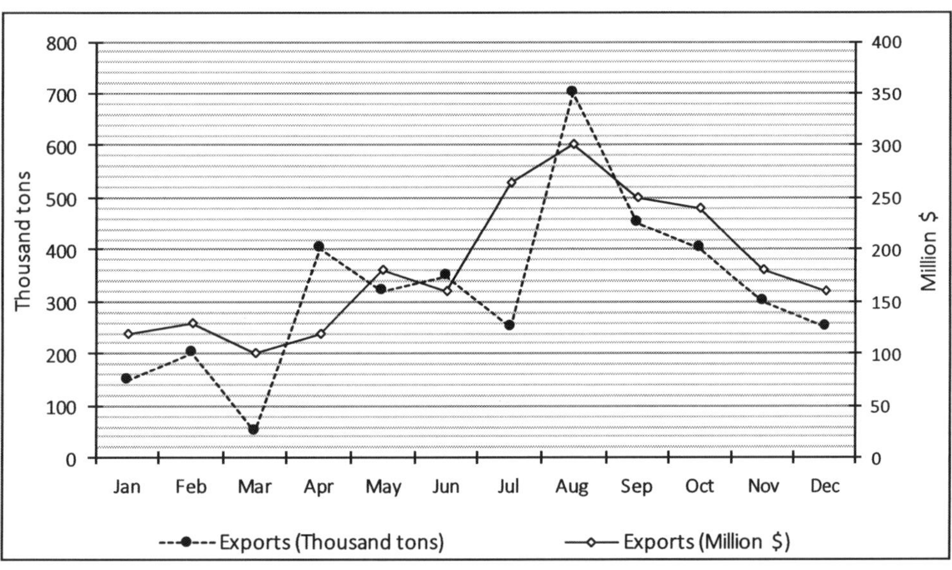

30. For Dec 2001:

Exports (volume)

= 260 thousand tons (see the left-side scale)

$= \left(260 \times 10^3\right)$ tons

Exports (revenue)

= \$160 million (the point is one small division above 150 mark, on the right-side scale)

$= \$\left(160 \times 10^6\right)$

Thus, the average price

$= \$\left(\frac{160 \times 10^6}{260 \times 10^3}\right)$

$= \$\left(0.61538 \times 10^3\right) = \$615.38$

The correct answer is option C.

31. Working with the options:

- Option A: February = 200, March = 50 => Percent decrease = $\frac{200 - 50}{200} \times 100 = 75\%$
- Option B: April = 400, May = 320 => Percent decrease = $\frac{400 - 320}{400} \times 100 = 20\%$

- Option C: June = 350, July = 250 => Percent decrease = $\frac{350-250}{350} \times 100 = 28.6\%$
- Option D: August = 700, September = 450 => Percent decrease = $\frac{700-450}{700} \times 100 = 35.7\%$
- Option E: September = 450, October = 400 => Percent decrease = $\frac{450-400}{450} \times 100 = 11.11\%$

The correct answer is option A.

Alternate Approach:

We can observe that from February (200) to March (50), the export goes down by $\frac{50}{200} = \frac{1}{4}$; the closed contender to this period could be August (700) to September (450), but the ratio for it equals $\frac{450}{700} = \frac{1}{1.56}$. Since $\frac{1}{4} << \frac{1}{1.56}$, the percentage decrease is highest for February - March.

32. We need to determine the maximum price of iron-ore per ton.

Thus, we should search for a month, in which the sales by volume are low, while the sales by revenue are high.

The obvious two such months are March and July. Though for months: Jan, Feb, March, Sept, Oct, Nov, and Dec, the sales by revenue are more than the sales by volume, volumes are not relatively too low than their respective revenues, rendering not much higher values of price per ton.

- March:

  Exports (volume) = 50 thousand tons (the point is midway between the 0 and 100 mark, on the left scale) = (50×10^3) tons

  Exports (revenue) = \$100 million = \$ (100×10^6)

  Thus, the price per ton = \$ $\left(\frac{100 \times 10^6}{50 \times 10^3}\right)$ = \$2000

- July:

  Exports (volume) = 250 thousand tons (the point is midway between the 200 and 300 mark, on the left scale) = (250×10^3) tons

  Exports (revenue) = \$265 million (the point is $1\frac{1}{2}$ small divisions above 250 mark, on the right scale) = \$ (265×10^6)

  Thus, the price per ton = \$ $\left(\frac{265 \times 10^6}{250 \times 10^3}\right)$ = \$1060

Note: The 'approximate' price per ton for each month is shown below for your reference:

	Jan	Feb	Mar	Apr	May	Jun	Jul	Aug	Sep	Oct	Nov	Dec
Exports ('000 tons)	150	200	50	400	320	350	250	700	450	400	300	250
Exports ($ million)	120	130	100	120	180	160	265	300	250	240	180	160
Price per ton ($)	800	650	**2000**	300	563	457	1060	429	556	600	600	640

The correct answer is option E.

33. The values of the exports (thousand tons) in the above period, after arranging in ascending order are shown in the table below:

	Mar	Jan	Feb	Jul	Dec	Nov	May	Jun	Apr	Oct	Sep	Aug
Exports ('000 tons)	50	150	200	250	250	**300**	**320**	350	400	400	450	700

The median value is the average of the $\left(\frac{12}{2}\right)^{th} = 6^{th}$ term and the $\left(\frac{12}{2} + 1\right)^{th} = 7^{th}$ term

$= \frac{300 + 320}{2} = 310$ thousand tons

The correct answer is option B.

The following two questions are based on the following charts.

The graphs below show the profit (million dollars), revenue (million dollars) and the number of employees for XYZ Corporation for three years.

Expenditure in any year is calculated as the Revenue less the Profit.

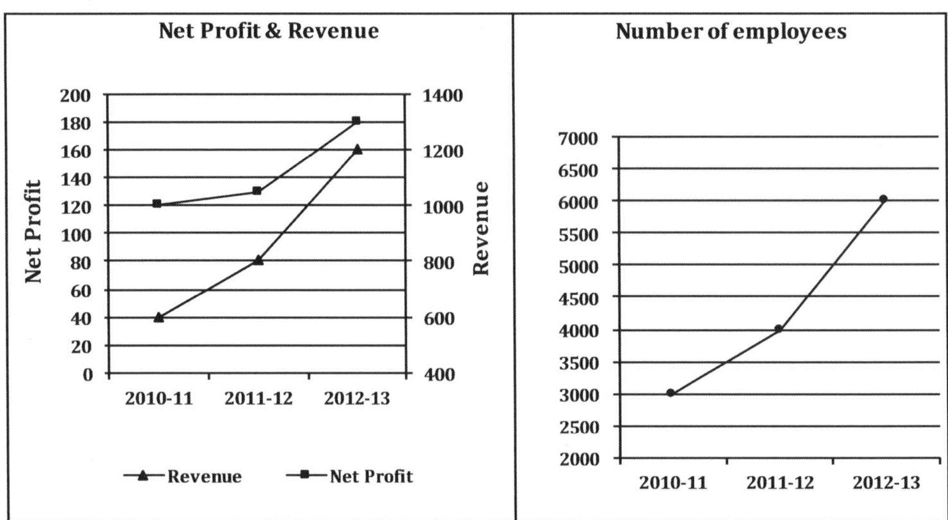

34. Expenditure in 2010-11 = \$ (600 – 120) million = $\$\left(480 \times 10^6\right)$

Number of employees in 2010-11 = 3000

Thus, average expenditure per employee in 2010-11 = $\$\left(\frac{480 \times 10^6}{3000}\right) = \$160,000$

Expenditure in 2011-12 = \$ (800 – 130) million = \$670 million

Number of employees in 2011-12 = 4000

Thus, average expenditure per employee in 2010-11 = $\$\left(\frac{670 \times 10^6}{4000}\right) = \$167,500$

Thus, percent increase in expenditure = $\frac{167500 - 160000}{160000} \times 100 = 4.7\%$

The correct answer is option B.

35. We know that the percent increase in the revenue (R) from 2011-12 (\$800M) to 2012-13 (\$1200M) is the same as that from 2012-13 to 2013-14.

The revenue became $\frac{1200}{800} = 1.5$ time from 2011-12 to 2012-13; thus, the revenue in 2013-14 would be 1200 × 1.50 = \$1800M.

Number of employees in 2013-14 is the same as that in 2012-13, i.e. 6000.

Thus, average revenue per employee in 2012-13 = $\$\left(\frac{1800}{6000}\right)$ million = \$0.3 million

The correct answer is option C.

The following two questions are based on the following chart.

The graph shows the sales and net profits of two companies, X and Y for four years. All figures are in billion dollars.

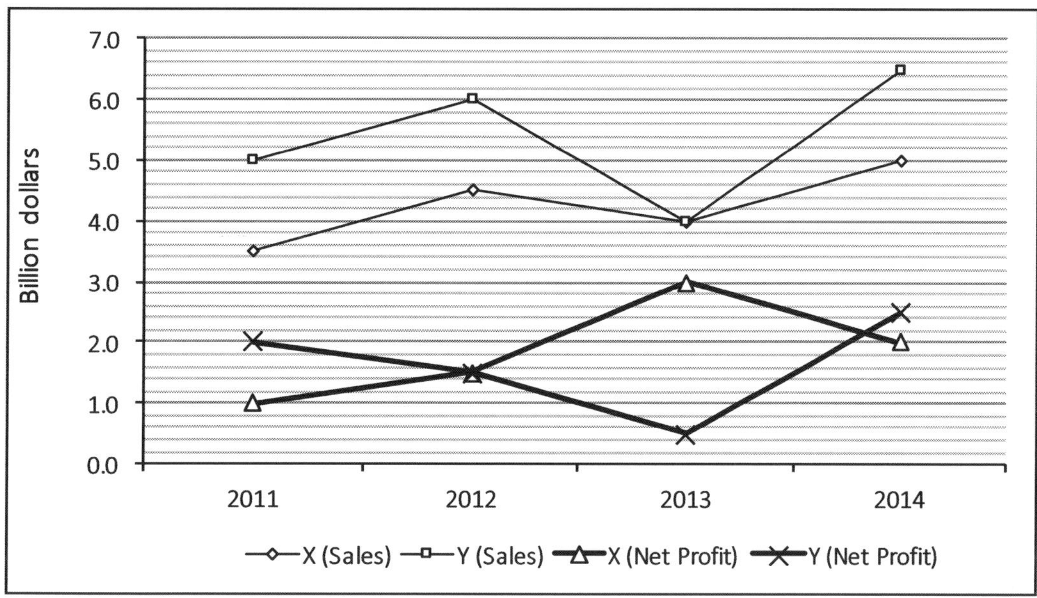

36. Calculating the ratio of net profit to sales for Company X for each of the given years:

- 2011: $\frac{\text{Net Profit}}{\text{Sales}} = \frac{1}{3.5} = \frac{2}{7} = 0.29$
- 2012: $\frac{\text{Net Profit}}{\text{Sales}} = \frac{1.5}{4.5} = \frac{1}{3} = 0.33$
- 2013: $\frac{\text{Net Profit}}{\text{Sales}} = \frac{3}{4} = 0.75$ (highest)
- 2014: $\frac{\text{Net Profit}}{\text{Sales}} = \frac{2}{5} = 0.40$

Alternately, we can easily observe that in 2013, the profit is the highest and the sales are the lowest. Hence, the ratio must be highest in 2013 equals to $\frac{3}{4} = 0.75$.

The correct answer is option C.

37. We need to determine the year(s) when:

Sales of X is lower than the sales of Y by more than 25%

$$=> \left(\frac{\text{Sales of Y} - \text{Sales of X}}{\text{Sales of Y}}\right) \times 100 > 25$$

$$=> \left(1 - \frac{\text{Sales of X}}{\text{Sales of Y}}\right) \times 100 > 25$$

$$=> 1 - \frac{\text{Sales of X}}{\text{Sales of Y}} > 0.25$$

$$=> \frac{\text{Sales of X}}{\text{Sales of Y}} < 0.75$$

Working with the options:

- Option A: In 2011: $\frac{\text{Sales of X}}{\text{Sales of Y}} = \frac{3.5}{5} = 0.70 < 0.75$ - Satisfies
- Option B: In 2012: $\frac{\text{Sales of X}}{\text{Sales of Y}} = \frac{4.5}{6} = 0.75 \nless 0.75$ - Does not satisfy
- Option C: In 2013: $\frac{\text{Sales of X}}{\text{Sales of Y}} = \frac{4}{4} = 1 \nless 0.75$ - Does not satisfy
- Option D: In 2014: $\frac{\text{Sales of X}}{\text{Sales of Y}} = \frac{5}{6.5} = \frac{10}{13} = 0.77 \nless 0.75$ - Does not satisfy

The correct answer is option A.

38. Since the pie-chart presents the percentage-wise revenue distribution, the total would be 100% for five sectors, thus the average revenue per year would be $\frac{100\%}{5} = 20\%$.

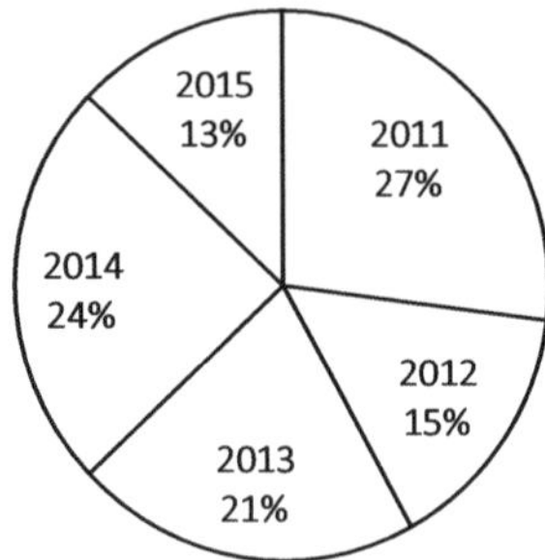

The closest figure to 20% in the pie-chart is 21%, thus the difference = 21% – 20% = 1%.
The difference of revenue 1% of \$125 million = \$1.25 million
The correct answer is option C.

The following three questions are based on the following chart.

Genre-wise percentage distribution of the Music-DVD market in Country X in 2010 is given in the pie-chart below. The Music-DVD market had a 60% share of the total music market, which was valued at $800 million.

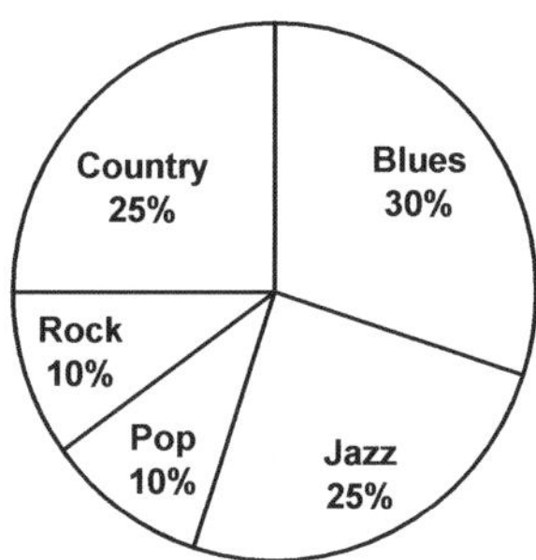

39. The music market = $800 million

Valuation of the Music-DVD market = 60% of $800 million = $480 million

Valuation of the music markets other than Music-DVD market = $ (800 – 480) million = $320 million

Share of Viacom-Music in Music-DVD market = 20% of $480 million = $96 million

Share of Viacom-Music in the music markets other than Music-DVD market = 5% of $320 million = $16 million

Thus, the market of Viacom-Music = $ (96 + 16) million = $112 million

The correct answer is option D.

40. Say, the the Music market in 2010 = $100 million

Market for Jazz in 2010 = 25% of $100 million = $25 million

Music-DVD market in 2010 = 120% of Music-DVD market in 2009

=> Music-DVD market in 2009 = (Music-DVD market in 2010) $\times \frac{100}{120} = 100 \times \frac{100}{120} = \frac{250}{3} \ldots$ (i)

Jazz market in 2010 = 150% of Jazz market in 2009

=> Jazz market in 2009 = (Jazz market in 2010) $\times \frac{100}{150} = 25 \times \frac{100}{150} = \frac{50}{3} \ldots$ (ii)

Thus, from (i) and (ii):

Required percent share = $\frac{\frac{50}{3}}{\frac{250}{3}} \times 100 = 20\%$

The correct answer is option B.

41. Let the Music-DVD market be \$100.

Thus, the percent values in the pie-chart represent the actual values of the market shares of the different genres.

Thus, the reported market value of Blues = 30% of \$100 = \$30

This value has been under-reported by 20%, i.e. this represents 80% of the actual value.

Thus, the actual market share of Blues = $\$\left(30 \times \frac{100}{80}\right) = \$37.5$

Thus, the actual share of Blues is \$7.50 greater than the reported value of \$30.

Since the values of the other genres remain unchanged, the total market would also increase from \$100 to \$107.50.

Thus, the actual percent share of Blues = $\frac{37.5}{107.5} \times 100 = 34.9\% =\approx 35\%$

(Note: Since the value of Blues would increase, the actual percent share of Blues would definitely increase, i.e. it would be greater than 30%)

The correct answer is option D.

The following two questions are based on the following tabular information.

Three machines produce capacitors for electrical circuits. The capacitors are inspected and either accepted or rejected. The following table gives the number of capacitors rejected and the percentage of the total production accepted for each machine:

Machine no.	Number rejected	Percent of production accepted
P	250	75
Q	308	78
R	248	68

42. We can express the data in a table as shown below:

Machine	Percent accepted	Percent rejected	Number rejected	Total produced
P	75	100 - 75 = 25	250	$250 \times \frac{100}{25} = 1000$
Q	78	100 - 78 = 22	308	$308 \times \frac{100}{22} = 1400$
R	68	100 - 64 = 32	248	$248 \times \frac{100}{32} = 775$
		Total	**806**	**3175**

Thus, total number of capacitors accepted = 3175 − 806 = 2369

Thus, percent of capacitors accepted = $\frac{2369}{3175} \times 100 = 74.6\%$

The correct answer is option E.

43. We can express the data in a table as shown below:

Machine no.	Number rejected	Percent accepted	Percent rejected	Production
P	250	75		
Q	**308**	78	100 - 78 = 22	$308 \times \frac{100}{22} = \mathbf{1400}$
R	248	68		

Let the cost of testing each capacitor produced by Machine Q be $\$x$

Number of capacitors produced by Machine Q = 1400.

Thus, total cost = $\$ (1400x)$

Total fine for each defective capacitor produced by Machine Q (at $0.50 per piece)

= $ (0.50 × 308) = $154

If one has to be indifferent to testing the circuits, the cost of testing should be the same as the fine applicable on the defective circuits.

Thus, we have:

$1400x = 154$

$=> x = 0.11$

The correct answer is option A.

Alternative Approach:

We see that for every 100 capacitors, 78 are accepted and thus, $100 - 78 = 22$ are rejected. If one chooses not to test the capacitors, the fine would be $\$0.50 \times 22 = \$11$.

To be indifferent to testing, the cost of testing 100 capacitors should be \$11, or \$0.11 per capacitor.

The following three questions are based on the following table and pie-charts.

The following table gives the number of families in a country in the years 2010 - 2013.

Year	No. of families (Millions)
2010	80
2011	85
2012	90
2013	95

The following charts give the distribution of families based on the number of members in a family for the years 2010 and 2013.

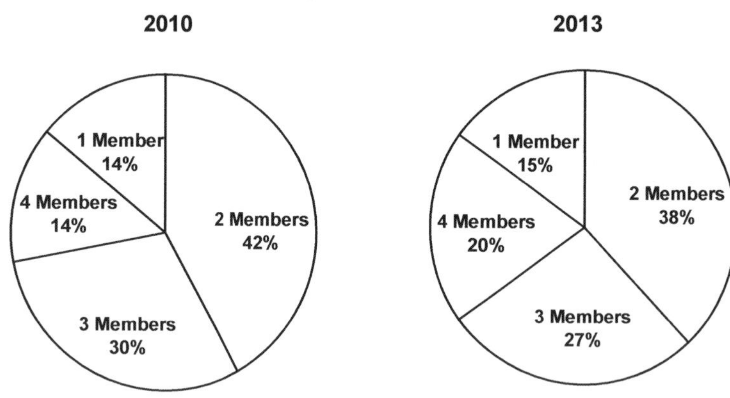

44. In 2010, we have:

- Number of families with 1 member = 14% of 80 million = 11.2 million

  Thus, number of members = $11.2 \times 1 = 11.2$ million

- Number of families with 2 members = 42% of 80 million = 33.6 million

  Thus, number of members = $33.6 \times 2 = 67.2$ million

- Number of families with 3 members = 30% of 80 million = 24 million

  Thus, number of members = $24 \times 3 = 72$ million

- Number of families with 4 members = 14% of 80 million = 11.2 million

  Thus, number of members = $11.2 \times 4 = 44.8$ million

Thus, total number of members = $11.2 + 67.2 + 72 + 44.8 = 195.2$ million

The correct answer is option D.

Alternate Approach:

We see that there are 14% families that have only one member in the family, thus their weightage for members = 14%; however, there are 42% families that have two members in the family, thus their weightage for members = $42\% \times 2 = 84\%$; the similar figures for 3 members is: $30\% \times 3 = 90\%$, and for 4 members is: $14\% \times 4 = 56\%$.

So, the total number of members in the families = $(14 + 84 + 90 + 56)\%$ of 80 million = 244% of 80 million = 195.2 million.

45. Number of 4-Member families in 2010 = 14% of 80 million = 11.2 million

Number of 4-Member families in 2013 = 20% of 95 million = 19.0 million

Thus, required percent increase = $\frac{19 - 11.2}{11.2} \times 100 = 69.6\% \approx = 70\%$

The correct answer is option D.

46. Let the total number of families in 2013 be 100.

Number of families originally having 1 member = 15% of 100 = 15

Number of families originally having 2 members = 38% of 100 = 38

Number of families having 1 member who married, and thus became 2-Member families

$= \frac{1}{3} \times 15 = 5$

Thus, the number of families having 2 members = $38 + 5 = 43$

Since the total number of families remains unchanged at 100, the required percent = 43%

The correct answer is option B.

The following two questions are based on the following table.

The following table provides the data on oil production and petrol production of five countries in 2010 and 2011. All figures are in million tons.

Country	Oil production		Petrol production	
	2010	**2011**	**2010**	**2011**
USA	40000	45000	5000	6000
China	18000	20000	3200	4500
India	25000	30000	4500	6000
Iran	80000	84000	10000	15000
UAE	90000	96000	25000	30000

47. Total oil production in 2011 by the five countries mentioned above

= 45000 + 20000 + 30000 + 84000 + 96000 = 275000 million tons

Total oil production in the world in 2011 = 450000 million tons

Thus, total oil production in the countries other than the five mentioned above in 2011

= 450000 − 275000 = 175000 million tons

Oil production by USA in 2011 = 45000

Thus, the required percent = $\frac{45000}{175000} \times 100 = 25.7\%$

The correct answer is option C.

48. The lowest petrol producing countries in 2010 are China and India.

Total petrol production of China and India in 2010 = 3200 + 4500 = 7700 million tons

Total oil production of China and India in 2010 = 18000 + 25000 = 43000 million tons

Thus, required percent = $\frac{7700}{43000} \times 100 = 17.9\%$

The correct answer is option C.

49. The highest petrol producing countries in 2011 are Iran and UAE.

Total oil production of Iran and UAE in 2011 = 84000 + 96000 = 180000 million tons

Total oil production of the five countries in 2011

= 45000 + 20000 + 30000 + 84000 + 96000 = 275000 million tons

Thus, required percent = $\frac{180000}{275000} \times 100 = 65.45\%$

The correct answer is option D.

The following two questions are based on the bar-graph and the line-graph below.

The chart below refers to three-year performance of the JP Chase Bank, in terms of Assets, in million dollars, and the number of Certificate Holders (CH), in millions.

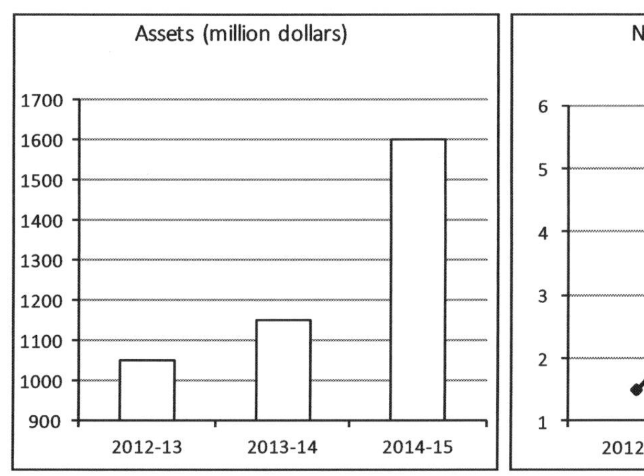

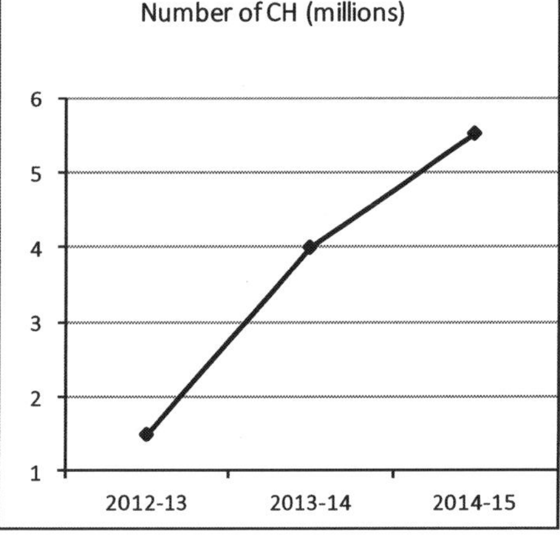

50. Number of certificate holders in 2014-15 = 5.5 million

Thus, expected number of certificate holders in 2015-16 = $5.5 \times 2 = 11$ million

Since the ratio of assets (in million dollars) to the number of certificate holders (in millions) has to be at least 320, we have:

$$\frac{\text{Assets}}{11} \geq 320$$

=> Assets $\geq$ \$ (11×320) million

=> Assets $\geq$ \$3520 million

Thus, the minimum value of assets should be \$3250 million.

The correct answer is option D.

51. Tax paid by the bank in 2014-15 at 6% rate = 6% of \$1600 million = \$96 million

Thus, tax paid by the bank in 2014-15 = \$96 million

Since the tax rate is 4%, we have:

4% of assets in 2015-16 = \$96 million

=> Assets in 2015-16 = \$ $\left(96 \times \frac{100}{4}\right)$ million = \$2400 million

The correct answer is option C.

Alternate Approach:

We know that tax = Asset $\times$ tax rate, and the tax for 2014-2015 and 2015-2016 should be the same. Since the tax rate is reduced to $\frac{4\%}{6\%} = \frac{2}{3}$ times, the asset for 2015-2016 should be $\frac{3}{2}$ times the asset in 2014-2015.

=> Assets in 2015-16 = $ $\left(1800 \times \frac{3}{2}\right)$ million = $2400 million

52. Since the mean of five integers is 10.2, the sum of the integers = $10.2 \times 5 = 51$

Let four of the five integers be 10 each.

Thus, the 5th integer = $51 - 4 \times 10 = 11$

Thus, the integers are: 10, 10, 10, 10 and 11, but their LCM is 110, not 12.

Since the LCM is 12, none of the numbers can exceed 12.

Also, since $12 = 2^2 \times 3$, none of the numbers can have a factor having an exponent of 2 greater than 2 or an exponent of 3 greater than 1. Thus, none of the numbers can be 8 or 9.

Also, none of the numbers can have factors other than 2 or 3. Thus, none of the numbers can be 5, 7, 10 or 11.

Thus, the only numbers that can be used are 1, 2, 3, 4, 6 and 12.

Since the mean of the numbers is 10.2, we must include numbers greater than 10.2; thus, one or more of the numbers must be 12.

Let us assume that the integers are 12, 12, 12, 12, and 3.

Since 3 is a factor of 12, the LCM is 12.

Thus, the required range = $12 - 3 = 9$.

Since this is a 'Could be true' type of question, we need not check for more possibilities.

The correct answer is option C.

53. We know that $a > b$ and that a and b are positive integers.

Thus, we have: $a^2b > ab^2$

Also, we have: $a^2 > ab > b^2$

We also have: $a^2b > a^2 > b^2$ and $ab^2 > b^2$

However, we cannot compare the values of ab^2 and a^2

(Note: $ab^2 > a^2 => b^2 > a$ and $ab^2 < a^2 => b^2 < a$; however, such conditions are not mentioned in the problem statement)

Thus, we have the possible scenarios for the five integers when arranged in order:

- $a^2b > ab^2 > a^2 > ab > b^2$

  => Median = $a^2 = 45 => a = \sqrt{45}$ - Not possible, since a is an integer

- $a^2b > a^2 > ab^2 > ab > b^2$

  => Median = $ab^2 = 45 = 5 \times 3^2 => a = 5,\ b = 3$ - Satisfies

Thus, the numbers, in descending order are: 75, 45, 25, 15 and 9.

=> Range = $75 - 9 = 66$

The correct answer is option D.

The following two questions are based on the following bar-graph.

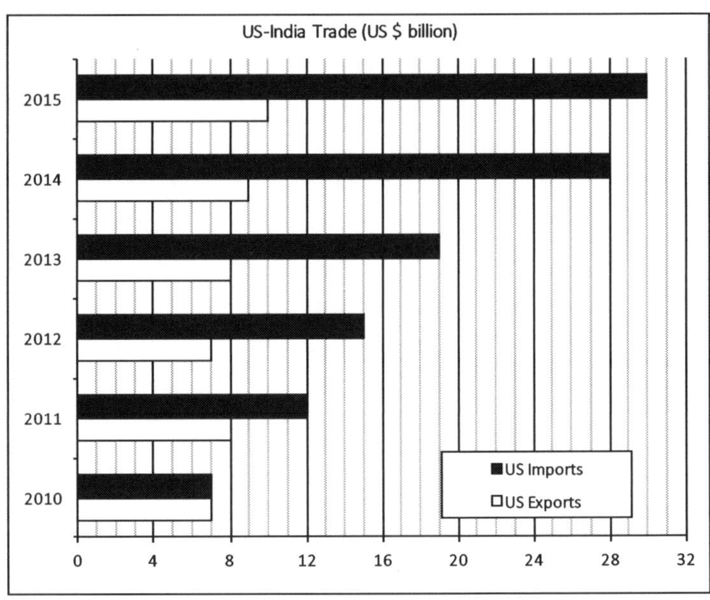

54. We need to determine the year in which the ratio of US exports to US imports was the minimum.

Thus, we should look out for the years for which US exports have lower values, and US imports have relatively much larger values.

From the bar-graph, it is clear that the year must be one among 2013, 2014 or 2015:

- Year 2013: $\frac{\text{US exports}}{\text{US imports}} = \frac{8}{19} = 0.42$

- Year 2014: $\frac{\text{US exports}}{\text{US imports}} = \frac{9}{28} = 0.32$ (Minimum)
- Year 2015: $\frac{\text{US exports}}{\text{US imports}} = \frac{10}{30} = \frac{1}{3} = 0.33$

The correct answer is option D.

55. US imports in 2011 = \$12 billion

US imports in 2015 = \$30 billion

Let the required rate of increase be $r\%$

The increase happened over four years: 2011 to 2012, 2012 to 2013, 2013 to 2014 and 2014 to 2015.

Thus, we have:

$30 = 12\left(1 + \frac{r}{100}\right)^4$

$=> \left(1 + \frac{r}{100}\right)^4 = \frac{30}{12} = 2.5$ Taking square root on both sides:

$\left(1 + \frac{r}{100}\right)^2 = \sqrt{2.5} = 1.58$ Taking square root again on both sides:

$1 + \frac{r}{100} = \sqrt{1.58} =\approx 1.26$

$=> r = 26\%$

The correct answer is option A.

5.2 Select One or Many Questions

56. Since 53% of the total people did not take juice, we can say that $(100 - 53) = 47\%$ of the total people took juice.

Let the number of people who took both be y and the number of people who did not take either drink be x.

Let us represent the above information using a Venn-diagram, as shown below:

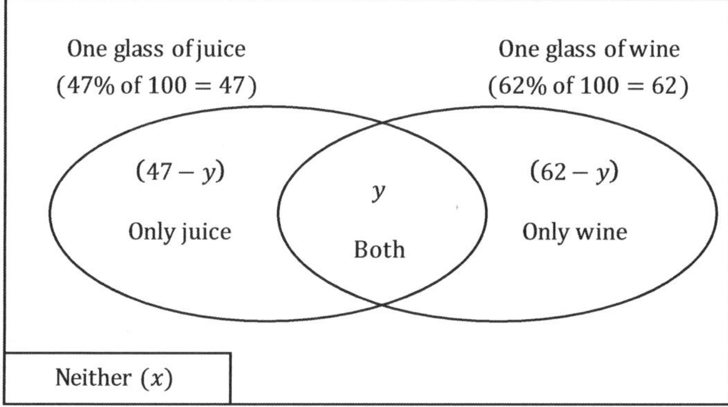

We know that 53% did not take juice

$\Rightarrow 62 - y + x = 53$

$\Rightarrow y = x + 9$

Since the value of x must be non-negative, we can say that:

$y \geq 9$

However, the value of y must be less than or equal to 47 (since the intersection of two sets must be less than or equal to the minimum of the individual sets).

Thus, we have:

$9 \leq y \leq 47$

Only options C, D, E and F satisfy the above condition.

The correct answers are options C, D, E and F.

57. We know that P is a set of consecutive positive integers from 1 to n.

Let us assume some values of n and calculate the required difference:

- $n = 4 : \text{P} = \{1,\ 2,\ 3,\ 4\}$
  Thus, we have:
  Even integers: 2, 4 => Median = $\frac{2+4}{2} = 3$
  Odd integers: 1, 3 => Median = $\frac{1+3}{2} = 2$

  => Difference in median = 3 − 2 = 1

- $n = 5 : \text{P} = \{1,\ 2,\ 3,\ 4,\ 5\}$
  Thus, we have:
  Even integers: 2, 4 => Median = $\frac{2+4}{2} = 3$
  Odd integers: 1, 3, 5 => Median = 3

  => Difference in median = 3 − 3 = 0

- $n = 6 : \text{P} = \{1,\ 2,\ 3,\ 4,\ 5,\ 6\}$
  Thus, we have:
  Even integers: 2, 4, 6 => Median = 4
  Odd integers: 1, 3, 5 => Median = 3

  => Difference in median = 4 − 3 = 1

- $n = 7 : \text{P} = \{1,\ 2,\ 3,\ 4,\ 5,\ 6,\ 7\}$
  Thus, we have:
  Even integers: 2, 4, 6 => Median = 4
  Odd integers: 1, 3, 5, 7 => Median = $\frac{3+5}{2} = 4$

  => Difference in median = 4 − 4 = 0

Thus, we observe that if n is even, the required difference is '1' and if n is odd, the required difference is '0'.

The correct answers are options A and B.

58. If we arrange the numbers (except x) in ascending order, we have: 1, 2, 4, 6, 18, 19, 20, 21

The middle two terms of the above set are 6 and 18.

Since the median value is x, there must be equal number of terms on either side of x.

Thus, x must be a number between 6 and 18, inclusive.

Thus, possible values of x are: 6, 7, 8, 9, 10, 11, 12, 13, 14, 15, 16, 17 or 18 . . . (i)

We know that the mean lies between 11.5 and 12.5.

Thus, we have:

$$11.5 < \frac{x + 1 + 2 + 4 + 6 + 18 + 19 + 20 + 21}{9} < 12.5$$

$=> 103.5 < x + 91 < 112.5 => 12.5 < x < 21.5$

Thus, possible values of x are: 13, 14, 15, 16, 17, 18, 19 20 or 21 . . . (ii)

Thus, from (i) and (ii), the possible values of x are 13, 14, 15, 16, 17 or 18.

The correct answers are options C, D and E.

59.

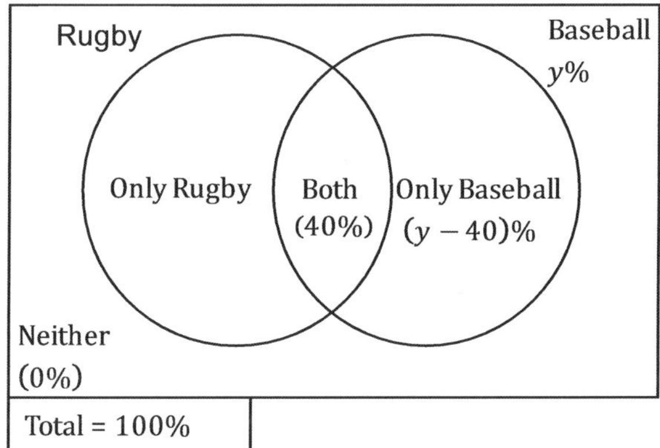

We know that 20% of the students who play baseball do not play rugby, i.e. play only baseball.

Thus, we have:

$y - 40 = 20\%$ of y

$=> y - 40 = \frac{y}{5}$

$=> y = 50$

Thus, percent of students who play baseball is 50% . . . Option A is correct (Option B is incorrect)

Sum of the values of the percent of students who play only Rugby and the percent of students who play Baseball (not only Baseball) is 100%.

=> Percent of students who play only Rugby
$= 100 - y = 100 - 50 = 50\%$ . . . Option C is correct

=> Percent of students who play Rugby
= Percent of students who play only Rugby + Percent of students who play both
$= 50 + 40 = 90\%$ . . . Option D is correct

The correct answers are options A, C and D.

60.

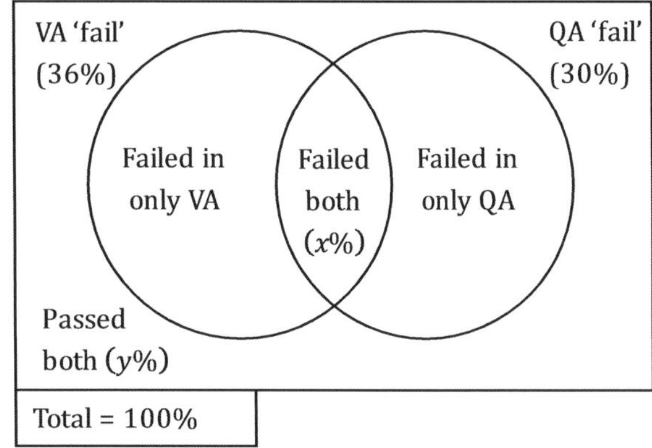

We have:

$36 + 30 - x + y = 100$

$\Rightarrow y = x + 34 \ldots$ (i)

Let us determine the maximum and minimum values of y.

From (i), the minimum value of y occurs when $x = 0$

$\Rightarrow y = 34$ (Minimum)

The maximum value of y will occur when the smaller set (QA fail) lies entirely inside the larger set (VA fail).

The corresponding diagram is shown below:

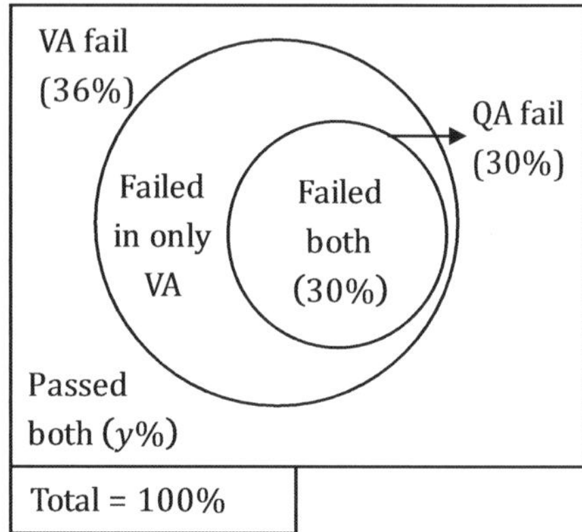

Thus, we have:

$y = 100 - 36 = 64\%$ (Maximum)

Thus, y lies between 34% and 64%, inclusive.

The correct answers are options C, D and E.

61.

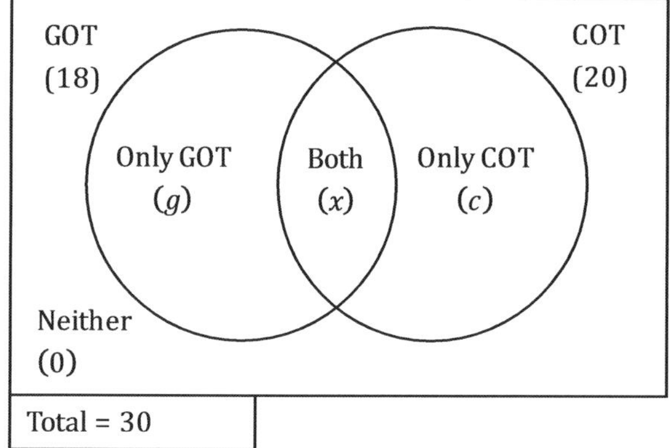

We have:

$18 + 20 - x = 30$

$=> x = 8$

Thus, 8 people liked both the shows . . . Option A is correct

$g = 18 - x = 10$

$c = 20 - x = 12$ . . . Option C is correct

Thus, number of people who preferred one show over the other

$= g + c = 22$ . . . Option B is correct

The correct answers are options A, B and C.

62.

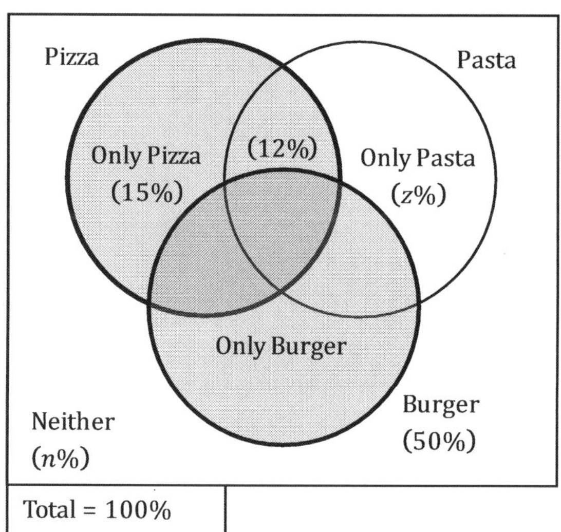

We need to determine the minimum and maximum values of the percent of students who like only pasta.

Pizza $\cup$ Burger = (Only Pizza) + (Only Pizza and Pasta) + (Burger) = 15 + 12 + 50 = 77%

=> $n + z = 100 -$ (Pizza $\cup$ Burger) = 100 – 77 = 23%

Since it has not been mentioned that every student likes at least one of the three types of food, and neither has the percent of students who like pasta been mentioned, we may easily minimize the percent of students who like only pasta to '0%' (to match the total students to 100%, the value of n can be adjusted to 23%).

Thus, the minimum percent of students who like only pasta is '0%' . . . (i)

Using the same reasoning as above, to maximize the percent of students who like only pasta, the value of n is minimized to '0%'.

Thus, the maximum percent of students who like only pasta is '23%' . . . (ii)

Thus, the percent of students who like only pasta lies between 0% and 23%, inclusive.

The correct answers are options A, B, C and D.

Following three questions are based on the following graph chart.

The graph shows the percentage of population owning TV sets in countries W, X, Y and Z.

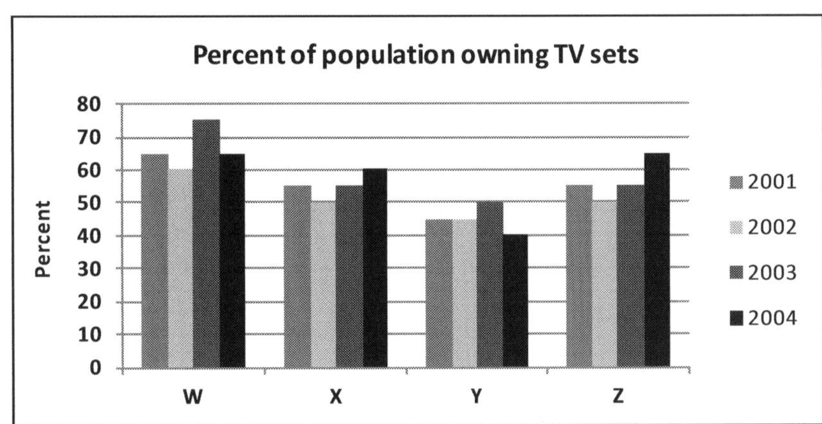

63. Since the population in a country remains the same across the years, the percent of viewership represents the actual number of viewers in the country.

Thus, we have:

- Percent decrease from 2001 to 2002 for W = $\frac{65-60}{65} \times 100 = 7.69\%$
- Percent decrease from 2001 to 2002 for X = $\frac{55-50}{55} \times 100 = 9.09\%$
- Percent decrease from 2001 to 2002 for Y = 0%

- Percent decrease from 2001 to 2002 for Z = $\frac{55-50}{55} \times 100 = 9.09\%$

Thus, the highest percent decrease is for countries X and Z.

The correct answers are options B and D.

64. Let the population in each country in each year be 100.

Thus, the percent of viewership represents the actual number of viewers in all the countries.

Let us work with the options:

- Option A: Percent increase from 2001 to 2004 for X = $\frac{60-55}{55} \times 100 = 9.09\%$ - Correct

- Option B: Both the number of TV sets in X in 2002 and in Y in 2003 are 50% of 100 = 50 - Correct

- Option C: Percent increase from 2001 to 2004 for Z = $\frac{65-55}{55} \times 100 = 18.18\%$
  Thus, average annual percent increase = $\frac{18.18}{3} = 6.06\%$ - Incorrect
  (Note: There are 3 years, not 4: 2001-2002, 2002-2003 and 2003-2004)

- Option D: Total number of TV sets in 2001 = 65 + 55 + 45 + 55 = 220
  Total number of TV sets in 2004 = 65 + 60 + 40 + 65 = 230
  Thus, percent increase = $\frac{230-220}{220} \times 100 = 4.55\%$ - Correct

The correct answers are A and B.

65. Let us work with the options:

- Option A: Let the population in Y in 2001 be 100
  Thus, the population in Y in 2002 = 110% of 100 = 110
  Population in Y in 2003 = 110% of 110 = 121
  Number of TV sets in 2001 = 45% of 100 = 45
  Number of TV sets in 2003 = 50% of 121 = 60.5

  Thus, required percent increase = $\frac{60.5-45}{45} \times 100 = 34.4\%$ - Correct

- Option B: It can be observed from the bar-graph that among all the countries, for the year 2001, the percent of people having TV sets is the least for Y. thus, it appears that the number of people with TV sets is the least for Y.

  However, the relative values of the populations of countries in 2001 are not known. Thus, the number of people owning TV sets in the countries cannot be compared.

For example, if the population of Y was 200, while that of X was 100, then number of TV sets in Y would be 45% of 200 = 90, while that in X would be 55% of 100 = 55.

Thus, the number of TV sets in Y need not be the lowest among all countries. - Incorrect

- Option C: Let the population in W in 2003 be 100
  Thus, the population in W in 2004 = 110% of 100 = 110
  Number of TV sets in 2003 = 75% of 100 = 75
  Number of TV sets in 2004 = 65% of 110 = 71.5

  Thus, required percent decrease = $\frac{75 - 71.5}{75} \times 100 = 4.7\%$ - Correct

The correct answers are options A and C.

66. Since there are 5 numbers, the median is the $\left(\frac{5+1}{2}\right)^{th}$ term, i.e. the 3rd term after arranging the terms in order. Thus, the middlemost number (after arranging the numbers in order) must be 5.

Also, since the range is 5, if the smallest term is x, the largest term is $(x + 5)$.

Thus, let the numbers after arranging in order be: $x,\ y,\ 5,\ z,\ (x+5)$

Since the numbers are distinct positive integers and there are 5 such numbers with the range being 5, we can have the following scenarios for the numbers:

- 3, 4, 5, 6, 8 => Mean = $\frac{3+4+5+6+8}{5} = 5.2 > 5$ - Satisfies
- 3, 4, 5, 7, 8 => Mean = $\frac{3+4+5+7+8}{5} = 5.4 > 5$ - Satisfies
- 2, 3, 5, 6, 7 => Mean = $\frac{2+3+5+6+7}{5} = 4.6 < 5$ - Does not satisfy
- 2, 4, 5, 6, 7 => Mean = $\frac{2+4+5+6+7}{5} = 4.8 < 5$ - Does not satisfy

Thus, the possible numbers in the set could be: 3, 4, 5, 6, 7 and 8.

The correct answers are options C, D, E and F.

67. If we arrange the numbers (other than a) in ascending order, we have:

3, 4, 7, 8, 11, 12, 13, 15, 22

Including a, there would be 10 terms. Hence, the median would be the average of the 5th and 6th terms.

11 must be either the 5th or the 6th term depending on the position of a.

The average of 8 and 11 is 9.5 (less than 10) while the average of 11 and 12 is 11.5 (greater than 10).

Thus, a must be either the 5th or the 6th term as well.

Thus, the median

$$= \frac{a + 11}{2} = 10$$

$\Rightarrow a = 9$

The correct answers are options A, B and D.

68. Let there be n numbers in set P, the numbers, in ascending order being $\{a,\ b,\ c, d,\ \ldots\ n\}$

Thus, the numbers in set Q are: $\{a + k,\ b + k,\ c + k,\ d + k,\ \ldots\ n + k\}$

The numbers in set R are: $\{ak,\ bk,\ ck,\ dk,\ \ldots\ nk\}$

Working with the statements:

- Option A: Since each term in set Q is increased by k, the total increases by $n \times k$ and hence, the mean must increase by $\frac{nk}{n} = k$.
  Thus, the mean of set Q is $(m + k)$ - Correct

- Option B: Since each term in set Q is increased by k, the smallest term would be $(a + k)$ and the largest number would be $(n + k)$.
  Thus, the range, which is the difference between the largest and the smallest numbers, would remain the same as r. - Incorrect

- Option C: Since each term in set R is multiplied by k, the smallest term would be ak and the largest number would be nk.
  Thus, the range, which is the difference between the largest and the smallest numbers, would become k times, equal to rk. - Correct

- Option D: Since each term in set Q is increased by k over that in set P, mean would also increase by k. Since the standard deviation is calculated using the deviation of each term from the mean, the deviation for each term would remain constant.
  Thus, the standard deviation would remain the same as s. - Correct

- Option E: Since each term in set R is multiplied by k over that in set P, mean would also be k times s. Since the standard deviation is calculated using the deviation of each term from the mean, the deviation for each term would also become k times.
  Thus, the standard deviation would become sk. - Incorrect

The correct answers are options A, C and D.

69. Let the five integers (the smallest one being 4) in ascending order be:

4, a, b, c and d

Since the mean is 8, we have:

$$\frac{4+a+b+c+d}{5} = 8$$

$=> 4 + a + b + c + d = 40$

$=> a + b + c + d = 36$

We need to determine the minimum and maximum value of d.

- The value of d is maximized if the values of a, b and c are minimized. Since the smallest number in the set is 4, the minimum value of a, b and c can only be 4.

  Thus, we have: $4 + 4 + 4 + d = 36 => d = 24$ (Maximum value)

- The value of d is minimized if the values of a, b, c and d are made equal.

  Thus, we have: $a = b = c = d = \frac{36}{4} = 9 => d = 9$ (Minimum value)

Thus, the value of d is between 9 and 24, inclusive.

The correct answers are options A, B, E, F, and G.

70. Since the question asks us to identify the statements which MAY be true, a possible approach can be using suitable numbers to check whether the statements may be true.

Working with the options:

- Option A: Since the numbers are not necessarily distinct, we can take all the numbers to be equal. In such an eventuality, the mean, median and mode will always be the same (equal to the numbers).
  For example, if the six numbers are a, a, a, a, a and a, each of mean, median and mode is also a.
  Thus, we have: $p = q = r$ - Option A may be true

- Option B: The set of numbers after arranging in order is: a, b, c, d, e, f
  Mean $= p = \frac{a+b+c+d+e+f}{6}$
  Median $= q = \frac{c+d}{2}$
  Thus, we have:
  $q > 3p => \frac{c+d}{2} > 3\left(\frac{a+b+c+d+e+f}{6}\right)$
  $=> c + d > a + b + c + d + e + f$

$=> a + b + e + f < 0$
This is not possible since the numbers are positive integers – Option B cannot be true

- Option C: Let the set of numbers after arranging in order be: 1, 1, 3, 5, 6, 14
  Mean $= p = \frac{1 + 1 + 3 + 5 + 6 + 14}{6} = 5$
  Median $= q = \frac{3 + 5}{2} = 4$
  Mode $= r = 1$
  Thus, we have: $p = q + r$ – Option C may be true

Note: The logic behind choosing such numbers: Since the mean is equal to the sum of the median and mode, we need to have a high value of the mean and relatively smaller values of median and mode. We arbitrarily choose 1 to be the mode. Also, to make the mean large, we use a large value for the largest number. The actual values of the numbers can be easily obtained by a little hit-and-trial.

The correct answers are options A and C.

5.3 Numeric Entry Questions

71. We need to determine the Inter-Quartile Range (IQR) of the 66 numbers.

The IQR is the difference between the Upper and Lower Quartiles of a set of data (IQR = Q3 − Q1), as shown in the diagram below:

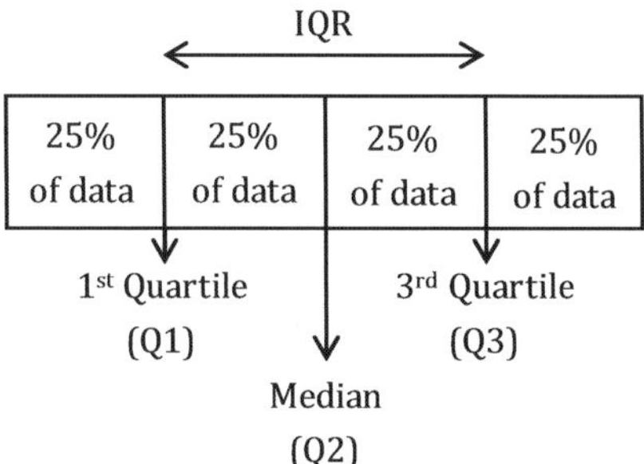

Thus, once the numbers are arranged in order, we have:

- Q1 = The median of the first 50% of the data.

  Since there are (50% of 66) = 33 numbers in the first half, we have:

  Q1 = The $\left(\frac{33+1}{2}\right)^{th}$ number

  => Q1 = The 17th number

- Q3 = The median of the last 50% of the data.

  Since there are (50% of 66) = 33 numbers in the last half, we have:

  Q3 = The $\left(\frac{33+1}{2}\right)^{th}$ number in the last half

  => Q3 = The $(33+17)^{th}$ number

  => Q3 = The 50th number

We know that the number of balls, n_i having a particular number i, painted on it is given by the relation $n_i = 3 + (i+1)^2$.

Thus, we have:

- For $i = 1$: Number of balls numbered '1' = $3 + (1+1)^2 = 7$
- For $i = 2$: Number of balls numbered '2' = $3 + (2+1)^2 = 12$
- For $i = 3$: Number of balls numbered '3' = $3 + (3+1)^2 = 19$
- For $i = 4$: Number of balls numbered '4' = $3 + (4+1)^2 = 28$

From the cumulative frequency table shown below, we have:

i value	Frequency	Cumulative frequency	
1	7	7	
2	12	7 + 12 = 19	**The 17th number => Q1 = 2**
3	19	19 + 19 = 38	
4	28	38 + 28 = 66	**The 50th number => Q3 = 4**

=> IQR = Q3 - Q1

= 4 - 2 = 2

The correct answer is '2'.

72. Let the five numbers be a, b, c, d and e (where $a > b > c > d > e$).

Since the average of the five numbers is 12, we have:

$$\frac{a+b+c+d+e}{5} = 12$$

$$=> a+b+c+d+e = 60$$

Since we have assumed $a > b > c > d > e$, the median of the five numbers must be the middle number, i.e. c.

Since the median of the five numbers is equal to $\frac{1}{3}$ of the sum of the four numbers other than the median, we have:

$$c = \frac{1}{3}(a+b+d+e)$$

$$=> c = \frac{1}{3}\{(a+b+c+d+e) - c\}$$

$$=> c = \frac{1}{3}(60 - c)$$

$$=> 3c = 60 - c$$

$$=> c = 15$$

Thus, the median is 15.

The correct answer is '15'.

73. Let the four numbers be a, b, c and d, where $a < b < c < d$.

Since the average of the numbers is 30, we have:

$$\frac{a+b+c+d}{4} = 30$$

$$=> a+b+c+d = 120$$

We know that none of the four numbers is greater than 33.

The value of the smallest number, a will be the minimum if the other integers have the maximum possible values:

$=> b = 31, c = 32$ and $d = 33$

Thus, the minimum value of $a = 120 - (31 + 32 + 33) = 24 \ldots$ (i)

The value of the smallest number, a will be maximum if the values of the other integers are reduced as much as possible, thereby making all four numbers equal to 30.

However, the four numbers are distinct, so we need to adjust their values, resulting in the following two possibilities:

a	b	c	d
$30 - 2 = 28$	$30 - 1 = 29$	$30 + 1 = 31$	$30 + 2 = 32$
$30 - 2 = 28$	$30 - 1 = 29$	30	$30 + 3 = 33$

Thus, the maximum value of $a = 28 \ldots$ (ii)

Thus, the difference between the maximum and minimum values of the smallest number

$= 28 - 24$

$= 4$

The correct answer is '4'.

74. Let the scores be a, b, c and d, where $a < b < c < d$.

Since the range is 12, the highest score $= d = (a + 12)$.

In order to maximize his highest score, i.e. d, we need to maximize his lowest score, i.e. a.

Since the median score is 80, we can have each of the first three scores as 80:

$a = b = c = 80$

Thus, we have:

$d = a + 12 = 92$

Thus, the scores are: 80, 80, 80 and 92

However, the test scores are distinct. Thus, we need to adjust the scores in such a way that all conditions are satisfied.

Thus, we have:

a	b	c	d
80 - 2 = 78	80 - 1 = 79	80 + 1 = 81	78 + 12 = **90**

Thus, the maximum possible score is 90.

The correct answer is '90'.

75. Let the minimum score be x.

Since the range is 70, the maximum score = $(x + 70)$

Let the score in the third test be y

The mean of the three scores

$$= \frac{x + (x + 70) + y}{3} = \frac{2x + y + 70}{3}$$

The median score must be y

Since the mean is 10 greater than the median, we have:

$$\frac{2x + y + 70}{3} - y = 10$$

$=> 2x + y + 70 - 3y = 30$

$=> x = y - 20$

Thus, the lowest score is 20 less than the median score.

The correct answer is '20'.

76. Let the five distinct positive integers be a, b, c, d and e, so that $a < b < c < d < e$

Since the median is 20, we have:

$c = 20 \ldots$(i)

Since the mean is 20, we have:

$$\frac{a + b + 20 + d + e}{5} = 20$$

$=> a + b + d + e = 80 \ldots$(ii)

Since the value of c is 20, and we need to maximize the product of the five numbers, we need to maximize the product $(a \times b \times c \times d)$.

We know that for a given value of the sum, the product is maximized if the numbers are equal. (For example, if p, q, r are three numbers and $p + q + r = 6$, the maximum value of the product $(p \times q \times r)$ occurs when $p = q = r = \frac{6}{3} = 2$ and the value becomes $2 \times 2 \times 2 = 8$)

Proceeding using the above logic, we should have $a = b = c = d = \frac{80}{4} = 20$

However, we need to keep the numbers distinct as well. Thus, we should assign such values for a, b, c and d so that their values are as close as possible to each other and at the same time, they remain distinct.

Thus, we have:

- $b = c - 1 = 19$
- $d = c + 1 = 21$
- $a = c - 2 = 18$
- $e = c + 2 = 22$

Thus, the numbers are: 18, 19, 20, 21 and 22.

The product of the smallest and largest numbers is $18 \times 22 = 396$

The correct answer is '396'.

77. In a Normal-distribution, approximately:

- 68% of the distribution lies within one standard deviation (±1 SD) of the mean.
- 95% of the distribution lies within two standard deviations (±2 SD) of the mean.

The percent of the distribution to the left of each SD-value is shown below:

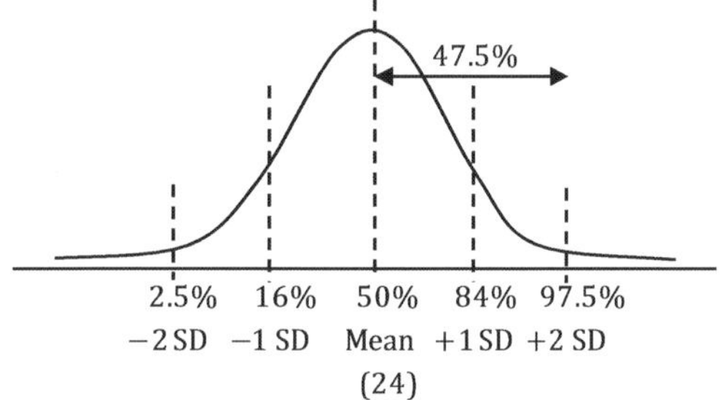

We know that the mean age is 24 years.

Also, 47.5% of the students have an age between 24 years and 28 years.

Thus, the value of the age, +2 SD from the mean is 28 years

=> SD of the ages = $\frac{28 - 24}{2}$ = 2 years

Thus, 20 years, i.e. (24 – 4) years is –2 SD from the mean and 22 years, i.e. (24 – 2) years is –1 SD from the mean.

Thus, the required percent of students 16% – 2.5% = 13.5%

The correct answer is '13.5'.

78. We know that the average age of all students is 15 years and that of the oldest three students is at least 17 years.

If we take the average of the oldest three students to be greater than 17 years, we would require more students having ages less than 15 years (average age of the class) to balance the higher age of the older students.

Since we need to minimize the number of students, we need to keep the average age of the older three students to be exactly 17 years.

We also know that no student is younger than 12 years.

Since 12 years is the least age possible, we assume the ages of the younger students to be exactly 12 years so that we need less students to balance the higher age of the older students.

Let the number of students 12 years old be x.

Since the average age of all students is 15 years, we have:

$$\frac{12x + 17 \times 3}{x + 3} = 15$$

=> $12x + 51 = 15x + 45$

=> $x = 2$

Thus, the minimum number of students = 2 + 3 = 5.

The correct answer is '5'.

79. Since the average of 5 integers is 65, the total = 65 × 5 = 325

The largest integer is 75

Thus, sum of the remaining 4 integers = 325 - 75 = 250

Thus, the average of the 4 integers would be = $\frac{250}{4}$ = 62.5

The smallest integer will be maximized if these 4 integers are as close to each other as possible.

Since the numbers are distinct integers, let us subtract 0.5 from the average (62.5) for one of the numbers and add 0.5 to the average (62.5) for the other number; giving us 62.5 - 0.5 = 62 and 62.5 + 0.5 = 63.

There are still two numbers left.

Let us subtract 1.5 from the average (62.5) for one of them and add 1.5 to the average (62.5) for the other; giving us 62.5 - 1.5 = 61 and 62.5 + 1.5 = 64.

Thus, the 4 integers are 61, 62, 63 and 64.

Thus, the maximum possible value of the smallest integer = 61.

The correct answer is '61'.

Alternate Approach:

Since we need to maximize the smallest number, we need to make the distance between the consecutive numbers minimum, in this scenario 1.

Let the smallest number be x, thus the 2nd smallest number = $(x + 1)$, and other numbers $(x + 2)$ and $(x + 3)$.

We have the sum of the above 4 numbers as 250.

$x + (x + 1) + (x + 2) + (x + 3) = 250$

$\Rightarrow 4x = 244$

$\Rightarrow x = 61$

80. Since the average contribution by 4 students was \$20, total contribution = \$(20 × 4) = \$80

To maximize the ratio of the amounts contributed by any two students, we need to maximize the contribution of one student and minimize the contribution by another student.

To minimize the contribution by any student, we need to maximize the contribution made by the other students. Since the contributions are different, we assume that the contributions made by 3 students are \$25, \$24 and \$23.

Thus, contribution (minimum) made by the 4th student = \$(80 - 25 - 24 - 23) = \$8

Thus, the required ratio = $\frac{25}{8}$

The correct answer is '$\frac{25}{8}$'.

81. Let the 12 terms be $t_1,\ t_2,\ t_3,\ \ldots\ t_{12}$

Since the mean is x, we have:

$$\frac{t_1 + t_2 + \cdots + t_{12}}{12} = x$$

$$=> t_1 + t_2 + \cdots + t_{12} = 12x$$

The new series is obtained by adding 1 to the 1st term, 2 to the 2nd term, and so on.

Thus, the new terms are:

$(t_1 + 1),\ (t_2 + 2),\ (t_3 + 3),\ \ldots (t_{12} + 12)$

Thus, the sum of the above terms

$$= t_1 + t_2 + \cdots + t_{12} + (1 + 2 + 3 + \cdots + 12)$$

$$= 12x + \frac{12\,(12 + 1)}{2}$$

Thus, the new mean

$$= \frac{12x + 78}{12}$$

$$= x + 6.5$$

Thus, the increase in the mean = $(x + 6.5) - x = 6.5$

The correct answer is option '6.5'.

Alternate Approach:

If we see only the increment part of the term, we find that they form an arithmetic progression: 1, 2, 3, 4 ... 11, 12.

The average (Arithmetic Mean) of an arithmetic progression =

$$\frac{1}{2} \times (\text{I term} + \text{Last term}) = \frac{1}{2} \times (1 + 12) = 6.5.$$

82. The sum of the numbers of the set

$$= x + y + (x + y) + (x - 4y) + xy + 2y$$

$$= 3x + xy = x\,(y + 3)$$

Thus, the mean

$$= \frac{x\,(y + 3)}{6}$$

Since the mean is $(y + 3)$, we have:

$$\frac{x\,(y + 3)}{6} = y + 3$$

=> $x = 6$

We know that: $x + 2y = 22$

=> $2y = 22 - 6 = 16$

=> $y = 8$

Thus, the terms are: $\{x, y, (x + y), (x - 4y), xy, 2y\}$

$= \{6, 8, (6 + 8), (6 - 4 \times 8), (6 \times 8), (2 \times 8)\}$

$= \{6, 8, 14, -26, 48, 16\}$

Arranging in ascending order, we have:

$\{-26, 6, 8, 14, 16, 48\}$

Thus, the median of the above 6 terms is the average of the 3rd and 4th terms

$= \frac{8 + 14}{2}$

$= 11$

The correct answer is '11'.

83. Since the average of 7 numbers is 12, the sum of the numbers $= 7 \times 12 = 84$.

Let the numbers, when arranged in ascending order, be a, b, c, d, e, f and g.

Thus, we have:

$a + b + c + d + e + f + g = 84 \ldots$(i)

Since the average of the 4 smallest numbers in this set is 8, we have:

$a + b + c + d = 8 \times 4 = 32 \ldots$(ii)

Since the average of the 4 greatest numbers in this set is 20, we have:

$d + e + f + g = 20 \times 4 = 80 \ldots$(iii)

(ii) + (iii) – (i):

$d = 28$

=> $a + b + c = 32 - 28 = 4$

$e + f + g = 80 - 28 = 52$

Thus, the required difference $= 52 - 4 = 48$

The correct answer is '48'.

Alternate Approach:

Subtract (ii) from (iii):

$(d + e + f + g) - (a + b + c + d) = 48$

$=> (e + f + g) - (a + b + c)$

$=>$ Sum of 3 largest numbers – Sum of 3 smallest numbers = 48

84. The numbers of marbles with the 5 people are: 23, 45, 51, 66 and 73

Thus, total number of marbles = 23 + 45 + 51 + 66 + 73 = 258.

We need to maximize the median value.

The median of 5 terms is the $\left(\frac{5+1}{2}\right)^{th}$ term = 3rd term.

Let the terms be arranged in ascending order.

Since the median has to be maximized, we need to maximize the terms following the median. Thus, we need to maximize the 3rd, 4th and 5th terms.

Thus, we minimize the 1st and 2nd terms, keeping them at 1 and 2, respectively.

Thus, the number of marbles with the other 3 people = 258 – 1 – 2 = 255.

Since the above 3 people have different numbers of marbles, let the numbers be a, $(a + 1)$ and $(a + 2)$.

Thus, we have:

$a + (a + 1) + (a + 2) = 255 => a = 84$

Thus, the numbers of marbles are: 1, 2, 84, 85 and 86 (the median is maximized).

Thus, the range = 86 - 1 = 85

The correct answer is ‘85’.

85.

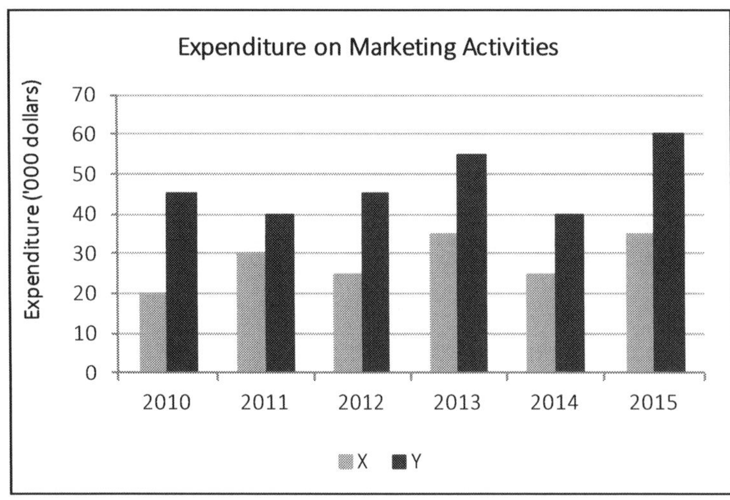

We can prepare a table for calculating the necessary values as shown below:

Year	Percent increase for X	Percent increase for Y	Ratio
2010 - 2011	**Not to be calculated, since there is a decrease for Y; we are interested in the increase for both X and Y.**		–
2011 - 2012	**Not to be calculated, since there is a decrease for X.**		–
2012 - 2013	$\frac{35-25}{25} \times 100 = 40\%$	$\frac{55-45}{45} \times 100 = 22.2\%$	$\mathbf{2 > \frac{40}{22.2} > 1}$
2013 - 2014	**Not to be calculated, since there is a decrease for X as well as Y.**		–
2014 - 2015	$\frac{35-25}{25} \times 100 = 40\%$	$\frac{60-40}{40} \times 100 = 50\%$	$\frac{40}{50} < 1$

Thus, the highest ratio was in 2012-2013, the corresponding value being:

$\frac{40}{22.2} = 1.8$

The correct answer is '1.8'.

5.4 Quantitative Comparison Questions

86.

Quantity A	Quantity B
The number of people in the group	8

Let the number of people who consumed tea and the number of people who consumed ice-cream be x and y, respectively.

Total number of calories consumed = $(3x + 240y)$.

Thus, we have: $3x + 240y = 966 \ldots$ (i)

Total cost of the food items consumed = $(5x + 20y)$.

Thus, we have: $5x + 20y = 90 \ldots$ (ii)

From $12 \times$ Eqn(ii) - Eqn(i), we have:

$57x = 114 \Rightarrow x = 2 \ldots$ (iii)

Substituting the value of x from (iii) in (ii):

$20y = 90 - 10 \Rightarrow y = 4 \ldots$ (iv)

Thus, from (iii) and (iv):

The number of people in the group = $(x + y) = 2 + 4 = 6$

Thus, Quantity B is greater than Quantity A.

The correct answer is option B.

87.

Quantity A	Quantity B
The median weight of the 89 boxes on these shelves	15 pounds

The median weight of 89 boxes would be the weight of the $\left(\frac{89+1}{2}\right)^{th} = 45^{th}$ box after the boxes have been arranged in increasing order of weight.

We know that each of the 45 boxes on shelf J weighs less than each of the 44 boxes on shelf K.

Thus, when all 89 boxes are arranged in ascending order of weight, the median weight, i.e. the weight of the 45th box will be the weight of the heaviest box on shelf J.

Since the heaviest box on shelf J weighs 15 pounds, we have:

The median weight = 15 pounds.

Thus, Quantity A is equal to Quantity B.

The correct answer is option C.

88.

If a variable is continuous, its probability distribution is called a continuous probability distribution.

For example, the value of a number between 0 and 5 is a continuous variable since the number can take any value like 2.19, 3.001, 4.0133, etc. However, the value of a number, which is an integer, between 0 and 5 is a discrete variable since it can only take the values 1, 2, 3, or 4.

A continuous probability distribution is different from a discrete probability distribution in the following ways:

- The probability that a continuous random variable will assume a particular value is zero. For example, the probability of choosing the number 3.12 in the above example is '0'.
- As a result, a continuous probability distribution cannot be expressed in tabular form. Hence, an equation (or graph) is used to describe a continuous probability distribution.

The equation used to describe a continuous probability distribution is called a probability density function, which has the following properties:

- The area bounded by the curve of the density function and the X-axis is equal to 1 (or 100 percent).
- The probability that the variable assumes a value between 'a' and 'b' is equal to the area under graph bounded by the lines $x = a$ and $x = b$.
- The median of such a distribution splits the area into two equal halves, with 50 percent of the area to the left of the median and the other 50 percent to the right of the median.

As verification, let us see if the area under the above curve is indeed equal to '1':

Radius of the above quadrant $= \frac{10}{9}$

Thus, the area of the above quadrant $= \frac{\pi \times \left(\frac{10}{9}\right)^2}{4} = \frac{3.24 \times \left(\frac{10}{9}\right)^2}{4} = 1$ (hence verified)

Quantity A	Quantity B
The median of the distribution of the variable V	$\frac{5}{9}$

In the given graph, let us draw a vertical line which divides the quadrant in two equal parts, as shown below:

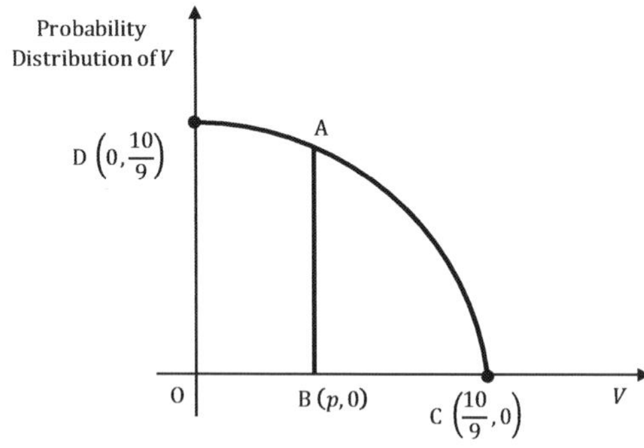

The median is the X-value of the coordinate of point 'B', i.e. 'p', in the above diagram.

Thus, to compute the median, we need to determine the length 'OB'.

We can clearly observe that the part of the area of the quadrant to the right of the line AB tapers off to meet the X-axis at C.

Thus, if a line $\left(A'B'\right)$ were drawn through the mid-point of the line OC, the area to the left of $A'B'$ would have been greater than the area to the right of $A'B'$, as shown below:

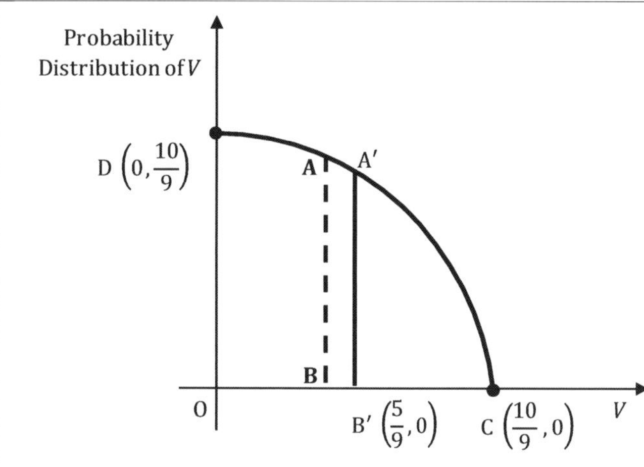

The X-value of the coordinate of point B′ would be the average of the X-values of the coordinates of the points 'O' and 'C' $= \frac{\left(0 + \frac{10}{9}\right)}{2} = \frac{5}{9}$.

Thus, in order to divide the area in two equal halves, the line $A'B'$ must be shifted more to the left to form the line AB instead.

Thus, the X-value of the coordinate of point B would be less than $\frac{5}{9}$.

Thus, the median of the distribution of the variable V is less than $\frac{5}{9}$.

Thus, Quantity B is greater than Quantity A.

The correct answer is option B.

89.

Quantity A	Quantity B
The greatest among the above 5 integers	94

Let the 5 distinct integers be: a, b, c, d and e, where $a > b > c > d > e$

Since the average of the 5 distinct integers is 17, we have:

$$\frac{a + b + c + d + e}{5} = 17$$

$=> a + b + c + d + e = 85 \ldots$ (i)

Again, since the least integer is -15, we have:

$e = -15 \ldots$ (ii)

Thus, from (i) and (ii), we have:

$a + b + c + d + (-15) = 85$

$=> a + b + c + d = 100 \ldots$ (iii)

Since the above integers are distinct, and we need to determine the greatest value of the integers, we minimize the values of b, c and d to maximize the value of a.

Since $e = -15$ is the smallest, we chose the following values:

$d = -14, c = -13$ and $b = -12$

Thus, we have:

$a + (-12) + (-13) + (-14) = 100$

$=> a = 100 + 12 + 13 + 14$

$=> a = 139$

Thus, the greatest value of the above 5 integers = 139.

Thus, Quantity A is greater than Quantity B.

The correct answer is option A.

90.

Quantity A	Quantity B
The greatest possible value of the smallest term	4

Since the average of the 5 distinct integers is 7, their sum

$= 5 \times 7 = 35$

There is a single mode of '9'.

Thus, '9' must be present more than once.

Since we need to maximize the smallest term, we need to keep all other terms as small as possible.

Thus, we assume that '9' is present exactly twice.

Also, we should have 9 to be the greatest term.

Thus, sum of the other three terms

$= 35 - (9 + 9)$

$= 17$

Since the smallest number has to be maximized, and there is a single mode, i.e. no other term can repeat (since 9 has been repeated twice), the other numbers would be:

4, 6 and 7

The best way of achieving the numbers is:

- We divide 17 by 3 (since 3 numbers add up to 17): $\frac{17}{3} = 5.67$
- This means that if each of the three numbers is 5, we still have 2 leftover
- Adding '2' to one of the three number, we have: 5, 5 and 7
- However, since no two numbers can be equal, we reduce '1' from one of the 5's and add '1' to the other, thus getting the three numbers as: **4**, 6 and 7.

Few possible combinations of values would be (3, 6, 8), and (2, 7, 8), but these are not the desired solutions as the questions asks for the maximum value of the smallest term.

Thus, the maximum value of the smallest term is 4.

Thus, Quantity A is equal to Quantity B.

The correct answer is option C.

91.

Quantity A	**Quantity B**
Twice the value of the greatest term	Thrice the value of the smallest term
We know that the average of 8 consecutive odd natural numbers is 36. The average of 8 consecutive odd integers (i.e. integers having a constant gap between each other) must be the average of the middle two terms, i.e. the 4th and the 5th terms. Since the 4th and 5th terms are both consecutive odd integers, and their average is 36, the terms must be 35 and 37. Since the gap between any two consecutive odd integers is '2', the numbers are: 29, 31, 33, 35, 37, 39, 41 and 43 Thus, the greatest number is 43 and the least number is 29.	
$2 \times 43 = 86$	$3 \times 29 = 87$
Thus, Quantity B is greater than Quantity A. The correct answer is option B.	

92.

<u>Quantity A</u>	<u>Quantity B</u>
The median value of the Gross Profit	$20,000

From the table, we have:

Month	Expenditure ('000 dollars)	Revenue ('000 dollars)	Gross Profit ('000 dollars)
January	130	160	160 - 130 = 30
February	120	140	140 - 120 = 20
March	110	120	120 - 110 = 10
April	140	160	160 - 140 = 20
May	150	180	180 - 150 = 30

Thus, arranging the Gross Profit values in ascending order, we have:

Month	Gross Profit ('000 dollars)
January	30
February	20
March	10
April	20
May	30

Thus, Quantity A is equal to Quantity B.

The correct answer is option C.

93.

Quantity A	Quantity B
The maximum possible sum of the median numbers of the four groups	40
To have the maximum average of the median values of the four groups, we need to maximize the median in each group. This is possible if we maximize the last three numbers in each group (the last three numbers are in ascending order). Thus, we choose the marbles with the following numbers for the four groups: {1, 17, 18, 19, 20}, {2, 13, 14, 15, 16}, {3, 9, 10, 11, 12}, and {4, 5, 6, 7, 8} Thus, the median numbers of the above groups are 18, 14, 10 and 6, respectively. Hence, the maximum possible sum of the medians = 18 + 14 + 10 + 6 = 48.	
Thus, Quantity A is greater than Quantity B. The correct answer is option A.	

94.

Quantity A	Quantity B
The maximum value of $\left(\frac{r}{q}\right)$	$12\frac{1}{3}$

Since $10 > r > q > p > 2$, the median of the three integers is q.

Since the average of the five integers is three times the median, we have:

$$\frac{2 + p + q + r + 10}{5} = 3q$$

$$=> 2 + p + q + r + 10 = 15q$$

$$=> p + r + 12 = 14q$$

Dividing throughout by q, we have:

$$\frac{p}{q} + \frac{r}{q} + \frac{12}{q} = 14$$

$$=> \frac{r}{q} = 14 - \left(\frac{12 + p}{q}\right)$$

The value of $\left(\frac{r}{q}\right)$ would be the maximum if the value of $\left(\frac{12 + p}{q}\right)$ is the minimum, i.e. when p has the least value and q has the greatest value.

Since $10 > r > q > p > 2$, and all the numbers are integers, the least possible value of $p = 3$ and the greatest possible value of q is 8 (if we take $q = 9$, then r cannot be assigned any integer value).

Thus, we have:

The maximum value of $\left(\frac{r}{q}\right)$

$$= 14 - \left(\frac{12 + 3}{8}\right)$$

$$= 14 - \frac{15}{8}$$

$$= 12\frac{1}{8}$$

Thus, Quantity B is greater than Quantity A.

The correct answer is option B.

95.

Quantity A	Quantity B
The number of possible values that exist for the largest of the five integers	Ten

Let the five integers be a, b, c, d and e, such that $a > b > c > d > e$.

Since the average of five integers is 12, we have:

$$\frac{a + b + c + d + e}{5} = 12$$

$=> a + b + c + d + e = 60 \ldots$ (i)

Since the smallest integer is 4, we have:

$e = 4 \ldots$ (ii)

Thus, from (i) and (ii), we have:

$a + b + c + d$

$= 60 - 4$

$= 56 \ldots$ (iii)

The largest integer, a, will have the maximum possible value if the remaining three integers have minimum values.

Since all the integers are distinct, we assume the following values:

$d = 5, c = 6$ and $b = 7 \ldots$ (iv)

Thus, from (iii) and (iv), we have:

$a = 56 - (b + c + d)$

$= 56 - (5 + 6 + 7)$

$= 38$

Thus, the maximum possible value of the largest integer is 38.

The minimum possible value of the largest integer will occur when a, b, c and d are as close to one another as possible.

If all the integers a, b, c and d were equal, from (iii), we have the value of each

$$= \frac{56}{4} = 14$$

However, the numbers are distinct; hence, we need to adjust them so that their average remains 14.

Thus, we choose the numbers:

14 - 2 = 12, 14 - 1 = 13, 14 + 1 = 15, and 14 + 2 = 16.

Thus, the minimum possible value of the largest integer is 16.

Thus, the values of the largest integer can be any number from 16 to 38, inclusive.

Thus, the largest integer can attain (38 - 16) + 1 = 23 possible values.

Thus, Quantity A is greater than Quantity B.

The correct answer is option A.

96.

Quantity A	Quantity B
The median of the five integers	9

Since the average of the five integers is 10, we have:

$$\frac{2p + (2p + 1) + 3p + (4p - 1) + (4p + 5)}{5} = 10$$

=> $15p + 5 = 50$

=> $p = 3$

Thus, the numbers (in ascending order) are:

$2p = 6,\ 2p + 1 = 7,\ 3p = 9,\ 4p - 1 = 11$ and $4p + 5 = 17$

Thus, the median of the 5 numbers is the $\left(\frac{5+1}{2}\right)^{\text{th}}$ number, i.e. the 3rd number

= 9

Thus, Quantity A is equal to Quantity B.

The correct answer is option C.

97.

Quantity A	Quantity B
The standard deviation of the set {1, 5, 7, 19}	The standard deviation of the set {0, 5, 7, 20}

Standard deviation (SD) is a measure of deviation of items in a set with respect to their arithmetic mean (average). Closer are the items to the mean value, lesser is the value of SD, and vice-versa.

Arithmetic mean of the terms $= \frac{1+5+7+19}{4}$ $= 8$	Arithmetic mean of the terms $= \frac{0+5+7+20}{4}$ $= 8$

The arithmetic means for both sets are the same.

Also, for both sets, the elements 5 and 7 are present.

While the other two elements in the set for Quantity A are 1 and 19, the other two elements in the set for Quantity B are 0 and 20.

Thus, the elements in the set for Quantity A are relatively closer to its mean than those in the set for Quantity B are to its mean.

Thus, the standard deviation of the set for Quantity B is greater than that the standard deviation of the set for Quantity A.

Thus, Quantity B is greater than Quantity A.

The correct answer is option B.

98.

Quantity A	**Quantity B**
The range of the heights of the boys and girls taken together	10 inches

Range is a measure of dispersion of data. It is calculated as the absolute difference between the maximum and minimum data of a set.

We know that:

The range of heights of the boys = 10 inches.

The range of heights of the girls = 8 inches.

Let us take two examples to analyze the situation:

Ex 1:

Let the minimum height among all boys = x inches.
Thus, the maximum height among all boys = $(x + 10)$ inches.

Let the minimum height among all girls = $(x + 1)$ inches.
Thus, the maximum height among all girls = $(x + 1 + 8) = (x + 9)$ inches.

Thus, the minimum height among all students = x inches.
Also, the maximum height among all students = $(x + 10)$ inches.

Thus, range of heights considering all students = $(x + 10) - x = 10$ inches.

Thus, Quantity A is equal to Quantity B.

Ex 2:

Let the minimum height among all boys = x inches.
Thus, the maximum height among all boys = $(x + 10)$ inches.

Let the minimum height among all girls = $(x + 3)$ inches.
Thus, the maximum height among all girls = $(x + 3 + 8) = (x + 11)$ inches.

Thus, the minimum height among all students = x inches.
Also, the maximum height among all students = $(x + 11)$ inches.

Thus, range of heights considering all students = $(x + 11) - x = 11$ inches.

Thus, Quantity A is greater than Quantity B.

Thus, Quantity A can be 'equal to' or 'greater than' Quantity B.

Logically, since the range of heights for the boys is 10 inches, which is greater than that for the girls, which is 8 inches, the range of heights considering all students, can have a minimum value of 10 inches.

Thus, the relation between Quantity A and Quantity B cannot be determined.

The correct answer is option D.

99.

Quantity A	Quantity B
The fraction of test takers in the group who scored greater than 81	$\frac{1}{5}$

A normally distributed data is shown below:

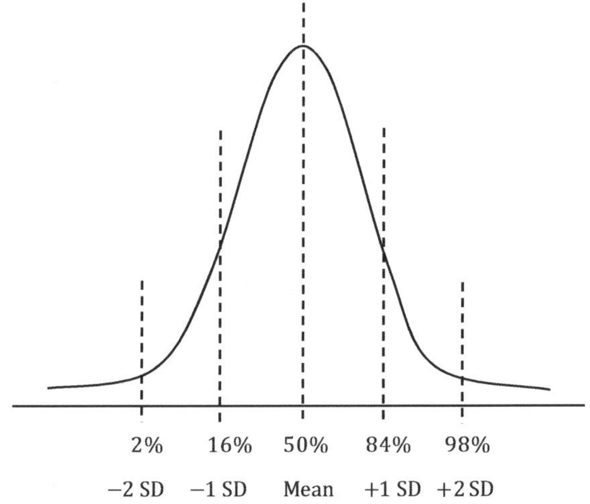

The required score, 81, is 81 - 74 = 7 greater than the mean score.

Since the standard deviation of the data is 4, the score 81 is $\frac{7}{4} = 1.75$ standard deviations away from the mean score.

Thus, we have the following diagram:

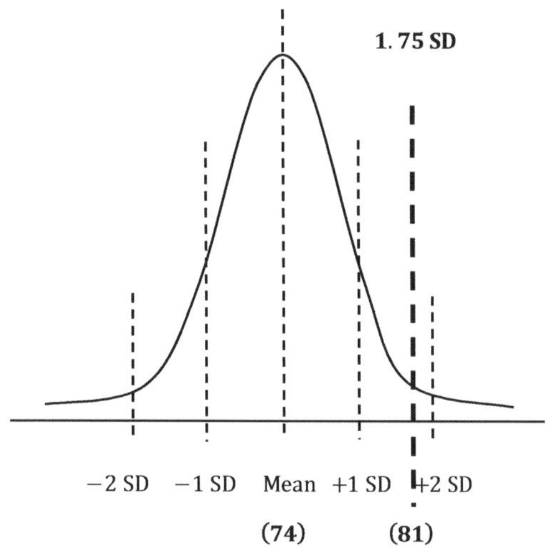

From the above diagrams, it is clear that the percent of the data to greater than '+1 SD' from the mean is 100 - 84 = 16%.

Thus, the percent of the data to greater than '+1.75 SD' from the mean must be much less than 16%. It is obvious that it would be much less than 20% = $\frac{1}{5}$.

Thus, the fraction of test takers in the group who scored greater than 81 is less than $\frac{1}{5}$.

Thus, Quantity B is greater than Quantity A.

The correct answer is option B.

100.

Quantity A	Quantity B
The average (arithmetic mean) of the smallest and the largest numbers	14

Let the four numbers be a, b, c and d (where $a > b > c > d$).

Since the average of the four number is 12, we have:

$$\frac{a+b+c+d}{4} = 12$$

$=> a + b + c + d = 48 \ldots$ (i)

Since we have assumed $a > b > c > d$, the median must be the average of the two middle numbers, i.e. $\left(\frac{b+c}{2}\right)$.

Since the sum of the four numbers along with their median is 58, we have:

$$a + b + c + d + \left(\frac{b+c}{2}\right) = 58$$

$=> 48 + \left(\frac{b+c}{2}\right) = 58 \ldots$ Using (i)

$=> \left(\frac{b+c}{2}\right) = 10$

$=> b + c = 20 \ldots$ (ii)

From (i) and (ii), we have:

$a + d = 48 - 20$

$=> a + d = 28$

Thus, the average of the smallest and the largest numbers

$= \frac{a+d}{2}$

$= \frac{28}{2}$

$= 14$

Thus, Quantity A is equal to Quantity B.

The correct answer is option C.

Chapter 6

Talk to Us

Have a Question?

Please email your questions to info@manhattanreview.com. We will be happy to answer you. Your questions can be related to a concept, an application of a concept, an explanation of a question, a suggestion for an alternate approach, or anything else you wish to ask regarding the GRE.

Please do mention the page number when quoting from the book.

GRE - Resources from ETS

- *Official Guide*: It is one of the best resource to prepare for the GRE revised General test. It is a complete GRE book with everything you need to do your best on the test — and move toward your graduate or business school degree. It includes a couple of full-length practice test and two simulated, computer-based GRE practice tests., which help you measure your capability beforehand. The book also includes a *POWERPREP II* CD.

- *GRE Big Book*: It is a big fat book and includes 27 previously administered full-length tests. There are over 5000 actual ETS questions and answers. The strategies and tips to crack the computerized GRE is worth reading.

Made in the USA
Las Vegas, NV
09 December 2021

36738778R00098